NUTSHELLS

TORT
IN A NUTSHELL

Other titles in the Series

Company Law
Constitutional and Administrative Law
Consumer Law
Contract
Criminal Law
English Legal Law
European Law
Family Law
Land Law
Trusts

AUSTRALIA
The Law Book Company
Brisbane ● Sydney ● Melbourne ● Perth

CANADA
Carswell
Ottawa ● Toronto ● Calgary ● Montreal ● Vancouver

AGENTS:
Steimatzky's Agency Ltd, Tel Aviv;
N.M. Tripathi (Private) Ltd, Bombay;
Eastern Law House (Private) Ltd, Calcutta;
M.P.P. House, Bangalore;
Universal Book Traders, Delhi;
Aditya Books, Delhi;
MacMillan Shuppan KK, Tokyo;
Pakistan Law House, Karachi, Lahore

NUTSHELLS

TORT
IN A
NUTSHELL

FOURTH EDITION

by
Ralph Tiernan, B.A.,
Senior Lecturer in Law,
University of Northumbria at Newcastle

London ● Sweet & Maxwell ● 1996

Published in 1996 by
Sweet & Maxwell Limited of
South Quay, Plaza, 183 Marsh Wall, London E14 9FT
Typeset by
Wyvern Typesetting Ltd, Bristol
Printed in England by Clays Ltd, St Ives plc
Reprinted 1996

A CIP Catalogue record
for this book is available
from the British Library

ISBN 0 421 548304

The index was prepared by Elisabeth Ingham

CONTENTS

1. Trespass to the Person   1
2. Negligence: Duty of Care   10
3. Negligence: Breach of Duty   28
4. Negligence: Damage   35
5. Contributory Negligence, *Volenti Non Fit Injuria* and *Ex Turpi Causa*   44
6. Liability for Dangerous Products   52
7. Employer's Liability at Common Law   61
8. Occupier's Liability   66
9. Breach of Statutory Duty   76
10. Defamation   81
11. Nuisance   92
12. Strict Liability   105
13. Liability for Animals   112
14. Vicarious Liability   119
15. Sample Examination Questions and Answer Plans   127

Index   137

1. TRESPASS TO THE PERSON

Trespass to the person may take one of three forms, namely assault, battery or false imprisonment. The action of trespass will lie for any direct and immediate interference with the plaintiff's bodily integrity and is actionable without proof of damage. It is doubtful that the defendant would ever have been liable where he was entirely blameless, but the burden of proof was at one time upon him to prove lack of fault (*Stanley v. Powell* (H.C., 1891)). In *Fowler v. Lanning* (H.C., 1959), however, it was held that the burden in an action of unintentional trespass to the person was on the plaintiff to prove negligence. This was approved in *Letang v. Cooper* (C.A., 1965) in which Lord Denning M.R. went so far as to suggest that where the interference is negligent, as opposed to intentional, the proper cause of action is negligence and not trespass. Support for this view is to be found in *Wilson v. Pringle* (C.A., 1986).

BATTERY

A battery may be defined as the direct and intentional (or possibly negligent) application of physical force to the person of another without lawful justification. It is the act of making physical contact which must be intentional and there is certainly no requirement of an intention to cause injury. Any physical contact, however trivial, may constitute "force" for the purposes of the tort notwithstanding the absence of bodily harm, subject to the proviso that the ordinary and sometimes inevitable physical contacts of everyday existence (*e.g.* jostling in a crowded place or touching a person for the purpose of engaging his attention) are not actionable. This qualification has been explained on the ground either that the plaintiff impliedly consents to such contact or, according to *Collins v. Wilcock* (H.C., 1984), that cases of this nature are to be treated as "falling within a general exception embracing all physical contact which is generally regarded as acceptable in the ordinary conduct of daily life." It was further held in *Wilson v. Pringle* (C.A., 1986) that the act must be "hostile" but, although this accords with the dictum in *Cole v. Turner* (1704) that the least touching of another "in anger" is a battery, no clear indication was given as to the meaning of hostile, save to say that it was not necessarily to be equated with ill-will or malevolence, the existence or otherwise of which was a question of fact. However, in *F. v. West Berkshire Health Authority* (H.L., 1989) Lord Goff doubted whether hostility was a requirement and opined that to hold otherwise would be difficult to reconcile with the principle that any touching of another's body is, in the absence of lawful excuse, a battery. Thus, he said, a prank which misfires, an over-friendly slap on the back, or surgical treatment in the mistaken belief that the plaintiff has consented, are prima facie actionable.

Apart from the more obvious examples of striking another with a fist or weapon, battery may take many forms. Thus, to spit in a man's face or to throw water over him, or to seize something from his hand, may be actionable wrongs. The defendant's act must be a positive one, voluntarily done; merely to obstruct the plaintiff's passage by standing still is not sufficient (*Innes v. Wylie* (1844)), just as there is no battery if the act is done in a state of complete automatism. However, in *Fagan v. Metropolitan Police Commissioner* (H.C., 1969) the defendant was held liable for criminal assault in respect of what appeared, on the face of it, to be a mere omission to act. The accused in that case accidentally drove his car on to the foot of a police officer and then deliberately delayed in removing the vehicle. One judge dissented on the ground that at the time of driving onto the officer's foot the defendant had no *mens rea*, and that after forming an intention to allow the car to remain there he did no positive act. The reasoning of the majority was that, where the defendant's act is a continuing one, the *mens rea* need not be present at the inception of that act but could, at some later time, be superimposed upon it.

One point which has still to be settled is whether the criminal law doctrine of transferred intent applies equally to the civil law. The problem arises where X, intending to strike Y, misses and hits Z by mistake; in these circumstances X commits a criminal offence but it remains undecided whether he would, in the absence of negligence, be liable in tort. In *Livingstone v. Ministry of Defence* (1984) the Northern Ireland Court of Appeal held that the doctrine does apply to a civil action.

As with all forms of trespass to the person the interference must be direct in the sense that contact with the plaintiff must follow immediately from the defendant's act. Thus, to place an obstruction in the plaintiff's path with the intention that he should trip over it may not be actionable as a trespass should the desired object be achieved, though there may be a remedy under the principle in *Wilkinson v. Downton* (H.C., 1897) (see later in this chapter). On the other hand, to strike a horse whereby its rider is thrown and injured has been held to constitute a battery (*Dodwell v. Burford* (1670)). The difficulties inherent in determining whether the interference is sufficiently direct are well illustrated in *Scott v. Shepherd* (1773). The defendant threw a lighted squib into a crowded market-place, whereupon it was thrown by two others acting in defence of their person and property until it struck the plaintiff in the face and exploded, causing him the loss of an eye. The defendant was, by a majority, held liable in trespass, but one judge dissented on the ground that the action should properly have been brought in case because the injury was consequential rather than direct.

ASSAULT

An assault may be defined as an act which directly and intentionally (or possibly negligently) causes the plaintiff reasonably to apprehend that a battery is about to be inflicted upon him by the defendant. Although the term assault is popularly used to include a battery, a person may be liable for an assault even though no battery is committed, for all that is required is the reasonable apprehension by the plaintiff of immediate violence. For example, to shake one's fist in another's face, or to aim a blow at him which is intercepted, is an assault, but the plaintiff must reasonably believe that the defendent has the means of carrying his threat into effect, so that there is no assault where the plaintiff is in such a position as to be inaccessible to physical force. Thus, in *Thomas v. National Union of Mineworkers* (H.C., 1985) there was held to be no assault when picketing miners made violent gestures to working colleagues who were being transported across the picket line under police escort. Just as there may be an assault without a battery, so there may be a battery without assault, as where the plaintiff is struck from behind, or whilst asleep, by an unseen aggressor. Even if the defendant is for some reason unable to carry out his threat or equally has no intention of so doing, there seems to be no logical reason why he should not be guilty of an assault, provided that his act induces in the plaintiff a reasonable apprehension that force is about to be inflicted upon him. A commonly cited illustration of this problem is that of pointing an unloaded gun at the plaintiff. In the civil case of *Blake v. Barnard* (1840) it appears to have been held that this would not constitute an assault, although the decision has been explained on the ground that the plaintiff, having averred that a loaded gun was pointed at him, then sought a verdict on the basis that it was unloaded. In the criminal case of *R. v. St. George*

(1840) the court was clearly of the view that it would be a common law assault to point an unloaded gun at the plaintiff (unless he knows it to be unloaded), and this would seem to be correct in principle.

As with battery there must be a positive act by the defendant, so that passive obstruction unaccompanied by any threatening move or gesture cannot amount to an assault (*Innes v. Wylie* (1844)). There is still doubt as to whether words alone may constitute an assault or whether some bodily movement is an essential requirement. In *Meade*'s case (1823) the view was expressed that "no words or singing are equivalent to an assault," but *dicta* in *R. v. Wilson* (H.C., 1955) point the opposite way. Whatever the position, words which accompany a threatening act may negative what would otherwise be an assault, as in *Tuberville v. Savage* (1669) where the defendant put his hand upon his sword and said: "If it were not assize-time, I would not take such language from you."

FALSE IMPRISONMENT

This may be defined as an act which directly and intentionally (or possibly negligently) places a total restraint upon the plaintiff's freedom of movement without lawful justification. The term "false" means wrongful and "imprisonment" signifies that the plaintiff has been deprived of his right to go where he will. Thus, a man may be imprisoned in his own home, in a motor car, or even in a public street, as long as his movements have been constrained by the defendant's will. Such constraint may be evidenced by the use of actual physical force amounting to an assault and battery, or simply by the reasonable apprehension of such force. But whilst the wrong of false imprisonment is often that of assault also, it is not necessarily so. For example, to lock a man in a room into which he has freely and voluntarily wandered is a false imprisonment but clearly not assault, although it is not clear whether a mere negligent lack of awareness of the plaintiff's presence in the room would suffice for the purposes of the tort.

The act of imprisonment

It has been seen that there need be no imprisonment in the ordinary sense of the word. An unlawful arrest is in itself a false imprisonment, as is the continued detention of one who, though originally in lawful custody, has acquired a right to be discharged. On the other hand, an arrest which is initially unlawful on the ground that no reason was given for the arrest may subsequently become lawful as from the time a reason is given (*Lewis v. Chief Constable of South Wales* (C.A., 1991)). The deprivation of the plaintiff's liberty must, however, be complete, and a mere partial interference with his freedom of movement is not an imprisonment. In *Bird v. Jones* (1845) the defendants wrongfully closed off part of a public footpath over Hammersmith Bridge. The plaintiff climbed into the enclosure but was refused permission to proceed and was told that he might make a detour by crossing to the other side of the bridge. There was held to be no false imprisonment. Provided the restraint is total, how large the area of confinement can be must depend on the circumstances of the case.

An imprisonment usually involves some positive act, and there is generally no duty to assist another to obtain his liberty. In *Herd v. Weardale Steel, Coke & Coal Co.* (H.L., 1915) the plaintiff miners wrongfully refused to do certain work in the mine and demanded that the defendants take them to the surface. The defendants refused for some 20 minutes to do so and, in an action for false imprisonment, it was held that the defendants' omission to accede to the plaintiffs' demands did not amount to an imprisonment. The plaintiffs had voluntarily accepted a restriction upon their liberty by initially going into the mine, and it was they who were in breach of contract by refusing to complete the shift. It may be that the defendants could have been liable had they been in breach of their own contractual duty. To similar effect is *Robinson v. Balmain New Ferry Co. Ltd* (P.C., 1910) where the plaintiff, having paid a penny to enter the defendants' wharf to catch a ferry, discovered that he had just missed one and wished to leave. He was directed to the exit turnstile where he refused to pay a further penny which, as was clearly stated on a notice–board, was chargeable upon leaving. It was held that there was no false imprisonment because the plaintiff had entered the wharf upon the terms of a definite contract by which the parties contemplated that he would take the ferry, and, since there was no agreement as to the terms on which he might go back, the defendants were not obliged to make the exit from their premises gratuitous but were entitled to impose a reasonable condition for the privilege.

There are numerous instances in which a person may voluntarily accept a degree of restraint upon his freedom of movement, but the above cases do not necessarily support the proposition that that person cannot thereafter revoke his consent and demand that the restraint be terminated, even though that would put him in breach of contract. Whether the defendant is obliged to comply with the demand will presumably depend, in particular, upon the degree of inconvenience caused in so doing.

A question which has recently been considered by the courts is whether a prisoner can be said to retain a degree of residual liberty such as to enable him to maintain an action against the prison governor for false imprisonment if he is further unlawfully restrained (*e.g.* by segregation from other prisoners in breach of the Prison Rules). The question received a negative answer in *Hague v. Deputy Governor of Parkhurst Prison* and *Weldon v. Home Office* (H.L., 1991). A prisoner can sue for torts committed against him by fellow prisoners or prison officers acting outside the scope of their authority, and, if subjected to intolerable conditions of detention which cause injury to his health, will have a private law remedy in negligence.

The defendant may be liable even though he does not personally detain the plaintiff, but only if the person making the arrest acts on the defendant's instructions and exercises no independent discretion. Where the police arrest on the basis of information received, they will almost undoubtedly be held to have exercised their own discretion, thereby relieving the informant of possible liability for false imprisonment. Thus, in *Davidson v. Chief Constable of North Wales* (C.A., 1994) a store detective's employers were held not liable to the plaintiff whom their employee had told police was guilty of theft.

The plaintiff's knowledge
In *Meering v. Grahame-White Aviation Co. Ltd* (C.A., 1919) it was held to be immaterial that the plaintiff was unaware of the fact of his detention, though this conflicted with the earlier decision in *Herring v. Boyle* (1834). In *Murray v. Ministry of Defence* (H.L., 1988) the House of Lords approved *Meering*, but expressed the view that a plaintiff who did not know of the detention would normally receive only nominal damages.

Means of escape
If a reasonable means of escape is available to the plaintiff there may be no false imprisonment. An escape route will very likely be unreasonable if it exposes the plaintiff to a risk of injury. If the plaintiff is unaware that such a route exists, the question is probably whether a reasonable man would have realised that there was an available outlet.

INTENTIONAL PHYSICAL HARM

Where the defendant wilfully does an act, or makes a statement, which is calculated to cause, and actually does cause, physical harm to the plaintiff, he is liable in tort. This statement of principle was laid down in *Wilkinson v. Downton* (H.C., 1897) where the defendant was held liable for falsely telling the plaintiff, by way of a perverted practical joke, that her husband had met with a serious accident, in consequence of which she suffered physical illness through nervous shock. This was approved in *Janvier v. Sweeney* (C.A., 1919) which also concerned a false statement causing shock, and both cases were relied upon in *Khorasandjian v. Bush* (C.A., 1993) as authority for the grant of an injunction where the defendant's campaign of harassment by means, *inter alia*, of threatening telephone calls was likely to injure the plaintiff's health, even though at the time of the action no damage had in fact been caused.

It is generally thought that there is no reason for restricting this principle to statements causing injury to the plaintiff's physical or mental health. Thus, to poison a man's drink or to set traps for him upon one's land (as in *Bird v. Holbrook* (1828)), or to infect him with a disease, may be actionable under this principle. It is doubtful whether such acts are trespasses because they are not sufficiently direct.

A difficulty which arises is as to the meaning of "calculated to cause harm." If this simply means that the harm was such that a reasonable man would foresee it as a probable result, then there would appear to be an overlap with the tort of negligence. Perhaps a more likely interpretation of the phrase is that the harm must be of a kind that the defendant actually contemplated or intended to produce, bearing in mind that an intention can be imputed where what follows from the defendant's act is a natural and probable consequence of it.

DAMAGES IN TRESPASS

All forms of trespass are actionable *per se* without proof of damage, though nominal damages only may be awarded where no actual loss is suffered. Aggravated damages may be awarded where, for example, an assault or battery takes place in humiliating or undignified circumstances and, in an appropriate case, exemplary or punitive damages may be awarded.

DEFENCES

The following defences are available in an action of intentional trespass to the person:

Consent

If the plaintiff expressly or impliedly consents to an act which would, but for that consent, amount to the commission of a tort, the defendant is not liable. Thus, the plaintiff may give his consent to physical contact within the rules of a lawful sport or to the performance of a surgical operation. Whether consent is an element of the tort or a defence properly so called is unclear. It was held in *Freeman v. Home Office (No. 2)* (H.C., 1983) that the burden of proof of lack of consent lay upon the plaintiff, but the more traditional view is that consent is a defence which the defendant must prove in the usual way.

Although consent is not a defence to a criminal assault, Lord Denning M.R. in *Murphy v. Culhane* (C.A., 1977) suggested that a person could, in an appropriate case, either be taken to have "assumed the risk" or be defeated by *ex turpi causa* (see Chap. 5). This might be so where, for example, the plaintiff was the aggressor and "got more than he bargained for." This view is further supported by *Barnes v. Nayer* (C.A., 1986), but it cannot apply where the defendant's response to the provocation is a "savage blow out of all proportion to the occasion" (*Lane v. Holloway* (C.A., 1968)).

In the context of medical treatment the principles applicable to the defence continue to evolve. Treatment without consent is prima facie a battery, and an adult of full mental capacity has an absolute right to choose whether or not to consent to treatment (*Airedale NHS Trust v. Bland* (H.L., 1993)). This right to self-determination was in issue in *Secretary of State for the Home Department v. Robb* (H.C., 1995) where, following *Airedale*, a declaration was granted that prison officials and nursing staff responsible for the care of a prisoner of sound mind who went on hunger strike could lawfully abide by his refusal to receive nutrition for so long as he retained the mental capacity to do so. In reaching this decision the court declined to follow *Leigh v. Gladstone* (H.C., 1909) which had held the forcible feeding of a suffragette justified on the ground of necessity. Where an adult patient is not in a fit state to give or withhold consent, a practitioner may nevertheless administer treatment either in an emergency, in which case he may rely on the defence of necessity (see below), or otherwise if he reasonably considers it to be in the best interests of the patient, though in this case he should seek the guidance of the court in the form of a declaration that the proposed treatment would not be unlawful. A minor of 16 or 17 may consent to treatment without parental approval (Family Law Reform Act 1969, s.8) as may a minor below that age, provided that he has sufficient intelligence and understanding to know precisely what is involved (*Gillick v. West Norfolk & Wisbech Area Health Authority* (H.L., 1986)). It seems, however, that no minor of whatever age can refuse medical treatment to which a parent has validly consented, and that the court can, in all cases involving minors, override the wishes of the patient in the exercise of its inherent wardship jurisdiction (*Re W* (C.A., 1992)).

Consent must be freely given and will therefore be vitiated if obtained by duress. It may also be invalid if obtained by fraud or misrepresentation, but only if the plaintiff is thereby mistaken as to the essential nature of the act. A mistake merely as to the consequences of the act does not affect consent, so that a patient need only be informed in broad terms of the nature of any proposed treatment (*Chatterton v. Gerson* (H.C., 1981)). Failure to disclose known risks associated with the treatment cannot therefore give rise to a battery but may be actionable in negligence (*Sidaway v. Governors of the Bethlem Royal Hospital* (H.L., 1985)).

Contributory negligence

In *Barnes v. Nayer* (C.A., 1986) it was considered that this could afford a defence in an appropriate case, but that it would not be available where the defendant's retaliatory act was wholly disproportionate to the plaintiff's misconduct.

Necessity

The basis of this defence is that the defendant was obliged to act as he did in order to prevent greater harm either to himself or a third party. The giving of emergency treatment to one who is unable to consent, for example, may be justified on this ground (*F. v. West Berkshire Health Authority* (H.L., 1989)). The defence is not available where the occasion of necessity is brought about by the defendant's negligence, and once this matter is raised it is for the defendant to show that he was not negligent (*Rigby v. Chief Constable of Northamptonshire* (H.C., 1985)).

Self-defence

A man may use such reasonable force as is necessary to protect himself or his property, and to prevent the entry of, or to eject, a trespasser upon his land. The use of reasonable force to prevent crime is statutorily sanctioned, so a defence is available to one who goes to assist another under attack.

Lawful arrest

This cannot be false imprisonment, nor will there be a battery by one who uses no more force than is reasonable to effect a lawful arrest. Detailed consideration of the law relating to powers of arrest, much of which is to be found in the Police and Criminal Evidence Act 1984, is not here possible; it is worth noting, however, that at common law any person may take reasonable steps to stop or prevent an actual or reasonably apprehended breach of the peace, and such steps may include the detention of a man against his will (*Albert v. Lavin* (H.L., 1982)).

---

2. NEGLIGENCE: DUTY OF CARE

Negligence as a tort may be defined as the breach of a duty of care, owed by the defendant to the plaintiff, which results in damage to the plaintiff. The concept of duty serves to define the interests protected by the tort of negligence by determining whether the type of loss suffered by the plaintiff in the particular way in which it occurred is actionable. The loss in question may arise through misfeasance or nonfeasance, and may consist of personal injury, damage to property, or what is categorised as pure economic loss. It may, in addition, consist of psychiatric damage (which was, until recently, more commonly termed "nervous shock") which has traditionally been treated as essentially different in kind to other forms of personal injury.

ESTABLISHING A DUTY

As the law developed it came to be recognised that certain relationships gave rise to a legal duty, such that carelessness by one of the parties in that relationship which caused damage to the other would entitle that other to bring an action for damages. In this way a number of specific "duty situations" were created, and the plaintiff had either to prove that his case fell within one of these existing categories of relationship or to persuade the court to recognise a new duty situation.

Forseeability and proximity and the "just and reasonable" requirement

In *Donoghue v. Stevenson* (H.L., 1932) Lord Atkin, in attempting to trace a common thread through existing authority, formulated a general principle – the "neighbour principle" – for determining whether, in any given case, a duty of care should exist. He said:

> "You must take reasonable care to avoid acts or omissions which you can reasonably foresee would be likely to injure your neighbour. Who then, in law, is my neighbour? The answer seems to be – persons who are so closely and directly affected by my act that I ought reasonably to have them in contemplation as being so affected when I am directing my mind to the acts or omissions which are called in question."

The significance of this principle was that it firmly established negligence as an independent tort and provided a basis for its expansion to cover situations not governed by precedent. This is not to say, however, that types of loss which were not recoverable prior to 1932 were thereafter compensable simply on the basis that such loss was reasonably foreseeable. Thus, the neighbour principle came to be applied where the plaintiff suffered personal injury or damage to his property as a result of the defendant's misfeasance but not, for example, where the loss was purely economic (see later in this Chapter).

Notwithstanding what has just been said there came a brief period where the boundaries of liability were extended to encompass claims which the courts had traditionally refused to entertain. This was largely as a consequence of the interpretation by some judges of the two-stage test propounded by Lord Wilberforce in *Anns v. Merton London Borough Council* (H.L., 1978) to mean that reasonable foresight of the particular damage in question (regardless of what form that damage might take) would give rise to a prima facie duty of care. The heresy of this approach was exposed by Lord Keith in *Yuen Kun Yeu v. Attorney-General of Hong Kong* (P.C., 1987) where his Lordship emphasised the need for a sufficient relationship of proximity between the parties which did not necessarily exist simply because damage was reasonably foreseeable. The expression "proximity or neighbourhood," he said, bore a wider meaning, importing the whole concept of necessary relationship between the parties, as envisaged by Lord Atkin when he spoke of neighbours as "persons who are so closely and directly affected by my act ..." His Lordship concluded that the term "proximity" was referable to "... such close and direct relations that the act complained of directly affects a person whom the person alleged to be bound to take care would know would be directly affected by his careless act." It must be understood that the term "proximity" in this context does not necessarily connote physical propinquity. Geographical proximity may be a relevant factor in determining the scope of the duty (see, *e.g., Home Office v. Dorset Yacht Co. Ltd* (H.L., 1970)), but there may clearly be "legal" proximity without physical proximity and vice versa.

In addition to the twin concepts of foreseeability and proximity there is yet a further requirement that it be just and reasonable to impose a duty upon the defendant (*per* Lord Keith in *Governors of the Peabody Donation Fund v. Sir Lindsay Parkinson & Co. Ltd.* (H.L., 1985); *Caparo Industries plc v. Dickman* (H.L., 1990)). Thus, in *Norwich City Council v. Harvey* (C.A., 1989) a sub-contractor was held to owe no duty to a building owner in respect of physical damage where, under the terms of the main contract, the permises were to be at the owner's risk. This case also illustrates the general reluctance of the courts to impose a duty of care in tort where the parties have come together against a contractural structure, the terms of which seek to define their rights and obligations, particularly where the imposition of such a duty would be inconsistent with those terms (see also, *e.g. Greater Nottingham Co-operative Society Ltd v. Cementation Piling and Foundations Ltd* (C.A., 1988); *Pacific Associates Inc. v. Baxter* (C.A., 1989)).

Public Policy

In an exceptional case public policy may militate against the imposition of a duty. Thus, the police owe no duty to an individual member of the public with respect to their function in the investigation and suppression of crime, on the ground that to hold otherwise would divert valuable resources from the performance of that function and would not promote the observance of a higher standard of care (*Hill v. Chief Constable of West Yorkshire* (H.L., 1988); *Alexandrou v. Oxford* (C.A., 1993); *Osman v. Ferguson* (C.A., 1993)). Similarly, it was held in *Hughes v. National Union of Mineworkers* (H.C., 1991) that, as a matter of public policy, senior police officers charged with deploying men to control serious public disorder were generally not liable to individual officers for alleged negligence in deploying an insufficient force. A further example of the role played by policy is to be found in the immunity enjoyed by advocates in the conduct of litigation (see later in this chapter).

Although the concept of public policy would seem to afford an independent ground for denying the existence of a duty, its relationship with the formal requirements remains something of a mystery. It was at one time thought, for example, that if the imposition of a duty would open the floodgates to litigation or expose the defendant tó a disproportionate liability, that was a sufficient policy reason for refusing to entertain the claim; but it is now more likely that the issue would be decided on the basis either of lack of proximity or that it would not be just and reasonable. Thus, Lord Oliver in *Alcock v. Chief Constable of South Yorkshire* (H.L., 1991) stated that ". . . 'policy', if that is the right word, or perhaps more properly, the impracticability or unreasonableness of entertaining claims to the ultimate limits of the consequences of human activity, necessarily plays a part in the court's perception of what is sufficiently proximate."

The present position
It should be noted that the question of whether the situation is capable of giving rise to a duty does not often cause a problem, since the majority of cases which come before the courts are covered by existing authority. It is clear from *Marc Rich & Co. AG v. Bishop Rock Marine Co. Ltd* (H.L., 1995), however, that in a novel case the three requirements (*viz.* foreseeability, proximity, and the just and reasonable criterion) must all be satisfied, regardless of the nature of the damage, in order for a duty to be owed. These formal requirements are inextricably interrelated, though the relative significance to be attached to each of them will very much depend upon the circumstances of the individual case, having regard in particular to the nature of the loss and the way in which it arises. Where, for example, positive conduct by the defendant inflicts physical harm on the plaintiff on his property, there can be little doubt that the mere foresight of such harm will, as a general rule, lead to the conclusion that there is a sufficiently proximate relationship and that the imposition of a duty would be just and reasonable (see, *e.g.* Lord Oliver in *Carparo Industries plc v. Dickman* (H.L., 1990), *Murphy v. Brentwood District Council* (H.L., 1990) and *Alcock v. Chief Constable of South Yorkshire* (H.L., 1991)). For an exceptional case in the context of property damage see *Marc Rich* (above). On the other hand, in the case of other loss or damage (*e.g.* economic or psychiatric), or where it is alleged that the defendant has failed to prevent damage by omitting to act (*i.e.* nonfeasance as distinct from misfeasance), the requirements of proximity and that it be just and reasonable to impose a duty assume a greater signi-

ficance and may have to be weighed more carefully in the balance. The relationship between these formal requirements is, however, by no means clear. In *Davis v. Radcliffe* (P.C., 1990) for example, Lord Goff said that proximity referred to such a relation between the parties as rendered it just and reasonable that a duty should be imposed, and Lord Oliver in *Caparo* suggested that lack of proximity could in some cases be attributed to a failure of the just and reasonable requirement.

Conclusion

The expansion of the scope of the duty of care in novel fact situations following *Anns* was halted by a series of decisions, many of them in the House of Lords, culminating in *Murphy v. Brentwood District Council* (H.L., 1990). The current thinking is that the law should develop incrementally by analogy with existing categories of duty situations, as propounded by Brennan J. in the Australian case of *Sutherland Shire Council v. Heyman* (1985) (see, *e.g. Caparo Industries plc v. Dickman* (H.L., 1990)). The concepts of proximity and what is just and reasonable, flexible and elusive as they are, have thus provided the courts with the tools with which to recognise or (as has much more often been the case of late) to deny the existence of a duty as they perceive the merits of the case to demand. However, following a sustained period of judicial reluctance to recognise new duties, there are now signs of a willingness to adopt a more flexible approach (see *Spring v. Guardian Assurance plc* (H.L., 1994)).

In short, in determining whether a duty of care exists in a novel case, an essentially pragmatic approach is adopted. As Lord Pearce observed in *Hedley Byrne & Co. v. Heller & Partners Ltd* (H.L., 1964):

> "How wide the sphere of the duty of care in negligence is to be laid depends ultimately on the courts' assessment of the demands of society for protection from the carelessness of others."

The remainder of this chapter deals with some of the more well established areas in which no duty, or a duty of limited scope only, has been held to exist.

ECONOMIC LOSS: NEGLIGENT MISSTATEMENT

Prior to *Hedley Byrne & Co. Ltd v. Heller & Partners Ltd* (H.L., 1964) liability for misstatements causing economic loss existed in the tort of deceit (*Derry v. Peek* (H.L., 1889)), in contract, or for breach of a fiduciary duty (*Nocton v. Lord Ashburton* (H.L., 1914)). The reluctance to impose liability in negligence was based principally on the "floodgates" argument, namely the fear of creating liability "in an indeterminate amount for an indeterminate time to an indeterminate class".

HEDLEY BYRNE

In this case the plaintiffs were advertising agents who wanted to know if they could safely advance credit to their client, X. The plaintiffs' bankers sought references from the defendants, X's bankers, who on two occasions replied, "without responsibility," giving favourable reports. The plaintiffs relied on the information and suffered financial loss when X went into liquidation. It was unanimously held that no duty arose because of the disclaimer, but that, in appropriate circumstances, a duty of care could arise. It was further agreed that reasonable foresight was not in itself sufficient because of the potentially far-reaching effect of the spoken word, and their Lordships thus spoke of the need for a "special relationship" before a duty would be owed. It appeared that such a relationship would exist where, to the defendant's knowledge (actual or constructive), the plaintiff relied upon the defendant's skill and judgment or his ability to make careful enquiry, and it was reasonable in the circumstances for him so to do. This relationship would now, to use the current terminology, be characterised as one of close proximity.

Subsequent developments

In *Caparo Industries plc v. Dickman* (H.L., 1990) Lord Bridge said that, in order for a duty to arise, it was necessary to show that the defendant knew that his statement would be communicated to the plaintiff, either as an individual or as a member of an identifiable class, specifically in connection with a particular transaction or transactions of a particular kind, and that the plaintiff would be very likely to rely on it in deciding whether or not to enter into the transaction. More recently, in *Henderson v. Merrett Syndicates Ltd* (H.L., 1994) it was held that where a person assumed responsibility to perform professional or quasi–professional services for another who relied on those services, the relationship between the parties was in itself sufficient to give rise to a duty on the part of the person providing those services. This broad statement of principle cuts across the traditional distinction (albeit one which is often none too clear) between negligent statements and negligent acts and explains, for example, why a solicitor may be liable in negligence to his client if he fails to issue proceedings within the relevant limitation period. Although in many instances the relationship between the parties will be contractual it was held in *Henderson* that this did not preclude the existence of a tortious duty.

Most of the cases have involved professional advisers, and the view of the majority in *Mutual Life and Citizens' Assurance Co Ltd v. Evatt* (P.C., 1971) was that the duty was limited to such persons, or to those holding themselves out as possessing a comparable skill and competence. The minority view, on the other hand, was that the duty would arise whenever a businessman in the course of his business gave information to a person who let it be known that he was seeking considered advice upon which he intended to act. This more liberal approach found favour in *Esso Petroleum Co. Ltd v. Mardon* (C.A., 1976), although the fact that the adviser is not in the business of giving advice of the type sought may be relevant in determining whether the plaintiff was reasonably entitled to rely on it for the particular purpose in question or whether, for example, he might reasonably have been expected to undertake further enquiries or obtain independent advice.

The application of Hedley Byrne

The defendant clearly need not know the identify of the plaintiff provided that he is aware of his existence either as an individual or as a member of an ascertainable class. A crucial ingredient of the duty is the defendant's knowledge (actual or constructive) of the purpose for which the information is required. In *Caparo Industries plc v. Dickman* (H.L., 1990) it was held that, in preparing the statutory audit of the accounts of a public company, the defendants owed no duty to the plaintiffs either as potential investors or as existing shareholders. The purpose of the audit was to report to the shareholders to enable them to exercise their rights in the management of the company, not to provide information which might assist them in making investment decisions. It follows from this that auditors owe no duty to existing or potential creditors of the company (*Al Saudi Banque v. Clark Pixley* (H.C., 1989), approved in *Caparo*). Similarly, it was held in *Al-Nakib Investments (Jersey) Ltd v. Longcroft* (H.C., 1990) that information in a prospectus inviting shareholders to subscribe for additional shares by way of a rights issue can be used only for that specific purpose, and not for the purpose of deciding to buy additional shares in the stock market (see also *James McNaughton Papers Group Ltd v. Hicks Anderson & Co.* (C.A., 1991)). The scope of the duty in these cases is thus restricted to situations which fall within the purpose for which the information is provided, so that where the defendant is specifically requested to prepare a report for the purpose of showing it to an actual or prospective bidder in a proposed take-over, there is no reason in principle why he ought not to be liable (*cf. Morgan Crucible Co. plc v. Hill Samuel Bank Ltd* (C.A., 1991); *Galoo Ltd v. Bright Grahame Murray* (C.A., 1995)). This may go some way to explaining the decision in *JEB Fasteners v. Marks, Bloom & Co.* (C.A., 1983), though in so far as a straightforward test of reasonable foresight was applied in that case it was held in *Caparo* to be incorrect.

In contrast to the position of auditors, surveyors appointed to value a house for mortgage purposes owe a duty to the purchaser even though the primary purpose of the valuation is to enable the lender to decide whether to advance a loan (*Yianni v. Edwin Evans & Sons* (H.C., 1982), approved in *Smith v. Eric S. Bush* (H.L., 1989) and *Harris v. Wyre Forest District Council* (H.L., 1989)). This has been justified on the basis that the valuer is paid for his services at the mortgagor's expense and must know that, in the case of a typical house purchase, the majority of buyers in fact rely upon his report and can not afford an independent valuation. The duty appears to be confined, however, to the person in respect of whose application the report is prepared and does not extend to subsequent owners of the property (*Smith v. Bush*). A warning note was also sounded in *Smith v. Bush* that the duty would not necessarily apply to commercial property or to houses at the more expensive end of the market, where the purchaser might be expected to obtain his own survey.

It is clear that *Hedley Byrne* does not apply to information or advice tendered "off the cuff" or on a purely social occasion, nor is there any general duty to volunteer information. The duty has been held to apply to pre-contractual negotiations (*Esso Petroleum Co. Ltd v. Mardon* (C.A., 1976)), though where the plaintiff is induced to contract as a result of a negligent misstatement he may, apart from a possible action in tort, sue under section 2(1) of the Misrepresentation Act 1967. The advantage of the statutory action is that the defendant has the burden of proving that he had reasonable grounds to believe, and did believe up to the time the contract was entered into, that the facts represented were true (see *Howard Marine & Dredging Co. Ltd v. A. Ogden & Sons Ltd* (C.A., 1978)).

Disclaimers and contributory negligence

Assuming that an appropriately worded disclaimer is brought sufficiently to the plaintiff's notice either before or at the time the statement is made, it could be argued that no duty arises because the plaintiff's reliance would not be reasonable. According to the House of Lords in *Smith v. Bush*, however, the effect of sections 11(3) and 13(1) of the Unfair Contract Terms Act 1977 is to subject all exclusion notices which would at common law provide a defence to an action for negligence, to a test of reasonableness, as provided for in section 2(2) of the Act.

Contributory negligence (see Chap. 5) is, in principle, a defence and is available equally to a claim under the Misrepresentation Act 1967 (*Gran Gelato Ltd v. Richcliff (Group) Ltd* (H.C., 1992)). The problem here is similar to that which arises in respect of disclaimers, namely whether a plaintiff who has himself been careless can be said reasonably to have relied upon the defendant, though an exceptional case is *Edwards v. Lee* (H.C., 1991) where the plaintiff, who had serious doubts about X's honesty, was held contributorily negligent in relying upon the defendant solicitor's reference on X. which failed to disclose that X. faced charges of fraud. On the issue of causation generally, the plaintiff must prove that the statement played a "real and substantial part" in inducing him to act (*JEB Fasteners v. Marks, Bloom & Co.*, per Stephenson L.J.).

Reliance by a third party

There are situations in which a duty of care will be imposed upon A. who makes a statement to B., as a result of which B. acts upon it to C.'s financial detriment. In *Ross v. Caunters* (H.C., 1980) for example, a solicitor who failed to inform his client, the testator, that the spouse of a beneficiary should not witness the will was held liable to an intended beneficiary for the loss of her bequest. Some doubt was cast on the decision in *White v. Jones* (H.L., 1995) where, however, a majority of the House of Lords held the defendant solicitors liable for failing to carry out their client's instructions regarding his will, with the result that the plaintiffs lost their legacy (*cf. Hemmeus v. Wilson Browne* (H.C., 1993)). The distinction between this case and *Ross v. Caunters* is that in this case the intended beneficiaries were clearly identified.

It has also been held that an employer supplying a reference about an employee to a prospective employer owes a duty to the employee to avoid making untrue statements negligently or expressing unfounded opinions, even if honestly held or believed to be true (*Spring v. Guardian Assurance plc* H.L., 1994)). In the opinion of the majority in *Spring* economic loss in the form of failure to obtain employment was clearly foreseeable if a careless reference was given and there was clear proximity of relationship as between employer and employee, so that it was fair, just and reasonable that the law should impose a duty on the employer.

ECONOMIC LOSS: NEGLIGENT ACTS

Although economic loss consequential upon injury to the person or to property has always been a recoverable item of damage, there is generally no liability for "pure" economic loss (see *Cattle v. Stockton Waterworks Co.* (H.L., 1875); *Weller & Co. v. Foot and Mouth Disease Research Institute* (H.C., 1966)). The distinction between pure and consequential economic loss is illustrated in *Spartan Steel & Alloys Ltd v. Martin & Co. (Contractors) Ltd* (C.A., 1973). The defendants negligently damaged a power cable, cutting off the electricity supply to the plaintiff's factory, as a result of which the plaintiffs suffered damage to their property together with loss of profit thereon, and pure loss of profit during the interruption to the supply. The plaintiffs succeeded in respect of the first part of their claim, but failed to recover for loss of profit which they would have made but for the power cut.

This arbitrary rule overcame the spectre of "liability in an indeterminate amount for an indeterminate time to an indeterminate class" (Cardozo C.J. in *Ultramares Corporation v. Touche* (1931)). However, although *Hedley Byrne*, which made a major inroad upon the principle that economic loss was not generally recoverable in tort, was originally confined to misstatements, there was a marked trend towards the formulation of a principle which would permit the recovery of economic loss in cases where there was no prospect of indeterminate liability (see, *e.g. Ross v. Caunters* (H.C., 1980)). The distinction between statements and acts (admittedly at times a very fine one) thus became blurred, and the highwater mark of this development came with *Junior Books Ltd v. Veitchi Co. Ltd* (H.L., 1983). This trend has been rapidly reversed of late, however, in consequence of the insistence of the appellate courts that the law should develop on an incremental basis by analogy with established categories of duty. It therefore seems that the law has reverted to its original state, namely that economic loss is normally irrecoverable unless the case can be brought within the parameters of *Hedley Byrne*.

Damage to third party property

In some cases physical damage to property belonging to a third party may prevent the plaintiff from carrying on his business (*e.g. Spartan Steel*, above). In other cases it will adversely affect his contract with the third party, rendering that contract less valuable or more expensive than expected (*Leigh & Sillavan Ltd v. Aliakmon Shipping Co. Ltd* (H.L., 1986); *Candlewood Navigation Corporation Ltd v. Mitsui OSK Lines Ltd* (P.C., 1986)). In neither case can the plaintiff recover because of the long-established rule that no claim will lie in respect of foreseeable economic loss, unaccompanied by physical damage to property in which the plaintiff has a proprietary or possessory interest.

Acquiring defective property

In this situation the plaintiff acquires ownership of property and subsequently discovers that it is defective, with the result that he must expend money in repairing or replacing it. Such economic loss, caused as it is by a defect in quality, may be recovered against a party who owes the loser a relevant contractual obligation, but has traditionally been regarded as irrecoverable in tort. The plaintiff cannot bring his claim within ordinary *Donoghue v. Stevenson* principles because that case is concerned with dangerously defective chattels which cause personal injury or damage to property other than the defective product in question (see Chap. 6).

This fundamental principle was seriously eroded by *Dutton v. Bognor Regis U.D.C.* (C.A., 1972) and *Anns v. Merton London Borough Council* (H.L., 1978), in both of which damages were held to be recoverable by a building owner against a local authority which had negligently inspected and approved defective foundations. Even if the damage (*i.e.* cracks in the fabric of the building caused by settlement) could be characterised as physical, that would still not come within the orthodoxy of *Donoghue v. Stevenson*, which had hitherto been confined to chattels causing damage to other property. Lord Wilberforce in *Anns* justified the decision on the basis that the cause of action arose when the building became an imminent danger to the health and safety of the occupier, who could then recover the cost of averting that danger. This novel development was taken a good deal further in *Junior Books* where the defendants were held liable for the cost of replacing a defective chattel supplied by them, even though there was no danger to health or safety. Although the decision was avowedly based upon the close proximity between the parties and reliance by the plaintiffs upon the expertise of the defendants, it went a considerable way towards recognising a general right of recovery for pure economic loss. Subsequent cases have made it abundantly plain, however, that it establishes no new principle and is to be confined to its particular facts. Furthermore, as a challenge to the hallowed belief that questions pertaining essentially to the quality of goods are to be resolved by reference to contractural obligations rather than to tort duties, the life of *Junior Books* has been brief (see, *e.g. Simaan General Contracting Co. v. Pilkington Glass Ltd (No.2)* (C.A., 1988), in which Dillon L.J. suggested that *Junior Books* had been the subject of so much analysis that future citation from it could not service any useful purpose). Thus, *Greater Nottingham Co-operative Society Ltd v. Cementation Piling and Foundations Ltd* (C.A., 1988) affirmed the traditional view that a duty could not be imposed in tort where to do so would be inconsistent with the contractual structure under which the parties had chosen to operate. This so-called contractual structure theory may equally apply where the loss is caused by a negligent misstatement (*Pacific Associates Inc. v. Baxter* (C.A., 1989)).

During the 1980s the duty imposed by *Anns* on local authorities was gradually restricted, so that it did not apply for the benefit of property developers or non-resident owners (*Governors of the Peabody Donation Fund v. Sir Lindsay Parkinson & Co. Ltd* (H.L., 1985); *Investors in Industry Commercial Properties Ltd v. South Bedfordshire D.C.* (C.A., 1986)). In *D. & F. Estates Ltd v. Church Commissioners for England* (H.L., 1988) the House of Lords clearly had difficulty in reconciling *Anns* with established tort principles. Lord Oliver thought that the decision was peculiar to the construction of a building, and agreed with Lord Bridge that it was logically explicable only on the ground that, in the case of a complex structure such as a building, the constituent parts could be treated as separate items of property distinct from that part of the whole which gave rise to the damage, thus bringing the issue within ordinary *Donoghue v. Stevenson* principles. For example, where defective foundations caused cracking in walls and ceilings, the latter could be regarded as "other property" for the purposes of an action.

This whole issue has now been considered by seven Lords of Appeal in *Murphy v. Brentwood District Council* (H.L., 1990). On similar material facts their Lordships unanimously overruled *Anns* in so far as it imposed a duty on local authorities, on the ground that where a defect in a building was discovered before any personal injury or damage to property other than the defective house itself had been done, the expense incurred by the building owner in rectifying the defect (or in vacating the premises) was pure economic loss and therefore irrecoverable in tort. In other words, once a dangerous defect is discovered it merely constitutes a defect in quality, and to permit recovery in tort would be to introduce a transmissible warranty of quality in the absence of any contract.

Although the decision is thought to be consonant with generally accepted theory of tort liability, it is not without difficulty. In the first place, whilst it would seem clear that a builder may be liable in accordance with *Donoghue v. Stevenson* principles where a latent defect causes personal injury or damage to other property, the question whether a local authority would also be liable was expressly left open. Secondly, Lord Bridge thought that where, after discovery of a dangerous defect, a building remained a potential source of injury to persons or property on neighbouring land or on the highway, the owner ought in principle to be able to recover in tort from the negligent builder the cost necessarily incurred (*e.g.* by repair or demolition) in order to protect himself from potential liability to third parties. Lord Oliver was unconvinced but reserved his opinion on the matter. Thirdly, the "complex structure" theory advanced in *D. & F. Estates* was regarded, at least by the majority, as unrealistic, because "the reality is that the structural elements in any building form a single indivisible unit of which the different parts are essentially interdependent." Lord Bridge then drew a distinction between a structural element which was dangerous only because it did not perform its proper function of sustaining the other elements, and a distinct item incorporated in the structure which positively malfunctioned, thereby causing damage to that structure. His Lordship gave examples of a defective central heating boiler which exploded and damaged a house, and of a defective electrical installation causing damage by fire, and said that if the damage was due to the negligence of the boiler manufacturer or of the electrical contractor the house owner could recover under *Donoghue v. Stevenson*. This, however, does no more than explain the position as it was long before *D. & F. Estates*. On the other hand Lord Jauncey considered that the complex structure argument might apply where a separate contractor had built an integral component of the structure, and a defect in that component caused damage to the structure, *e.g.* a steel frame failing to give adequate support to floors or walls.

Finally, and perhaps most significantly, their Lordships attached great weight to the fact that it is the plaintiff's *knowledge* of the defect which makes the defect one of quality only, and therefore the loss purely economic. But such knowledge has not in the past necessarily barred the right of recovery. Thus, in *Rimmer v. Liverpool City Council* (C.A. 1984) the local authority, who designed and built a council flat, was liable to a tenant injured by a pane of dangerously thin glass. The tenant knew of the danger and had complained about it, but it was considered that it was neither practicable or reasonable to expect him to leave, or to change the pane of glass himself (damages were reduced for contributory negligence). This was recently followed in *Targett v. Torfaen Borough Council* (C.A., 1992) where the facts were substantially similar. The defendants' argument that *Rimmer* had been overruled by *Murphy* was rejected by the Court of Appeal, who distinguished the latter case on the ground that the views expressed therein about the effect of the plaintiff's knowledge applied only to the type of claim in that case (*i.e.* pure economic loss) and not to a claim for personal injuries. According to their Lordships, knowledge of the defect would only negative the duty of care or break the chain of causation where it was reasonable to expect the plaintiff to remove or avoid the danger, or where it was unreasonable for him to run the risk of injury.

NERVOUS SHOCK

According to Lord Ackner in *Alcock v. Chief Constable of South Yorkshire* (H.L., 1991) shock "involves the sudden appreciation by sight or sound of a horrifying event, which violently agitates the mind." It must manifest itself in some recognisable psychiatric or physical illness; mere grief or emotional upset is not actionable, save that mental distress suffered as a result of negligently inflicted injuries may be taken into account in the assessment of damages for pain and suffering. Lord Ackner also made it clear that, as the law presently stands, there can be no recovery for psychiatric illness "caused by the accumulation over a period of time of more gradual assaults on the nervous system."

Adopting Lord Oliver's classification in *Alcock*, shock victims may fall into one of two broad groups, namely those who are unwilling participants in the events causing shock, and those who are merely passive and unwilling witnesses. With regard to the first group his Lordship said that if the defendant's negligent conduct foreseeably puts the plaintiff into that position it follows that there will be a sufficiently proximate relationship between them, though if personal injury of some kind to the plaintiff is reasonably foreseeable as the result of an accident the defendant is liable for psychiatric injury (even though no physical injury occurs), and like plaintiff need not prove that injury by shock was foreseeable (*Page v. Smith* (H.L., 1995)).

Into this group would fall such cases as *Dulieu v. White & Sons* (H.C., 1901) where the plaintiff recovered for shock induced by a reasonable fear for her own safety as a result of the defendant's negligence, and *Chadwick v. British Transport Commission* (C.A., 1967) where a rescuer at the scene of a railway disaster was held entitled to recover (though the mere fact that the plaintiff is a rescuer will not automatically entitle him to recover (*Frost v. Chief Constable of South Yorkshire* (H.C., 1995)); see Chap. 5). Similarly within the group are those cases where the defendant's negligence puts the plaintiff in the position of being, or believing himself to have been, the involuntary cause of another's death or injury (see, *e.g. Dooley v. Cammell Laird & Co. Ltd* (H.C., 1951); *Wigg v. British Railways Board* (H.C., 1986)).

However, where the plaintiff falls within the second of Lord Oliver's groups a more complex analysis is required. It was held in *Alcock* that in order to recover the plaintiff must prove the following;

(a) that his relationship to the primary victim was sufficiently close that it was reasonably foreseeable that he might suffer shock if he apprehended that the victim had been, or might be, injured:

(b) that he was temporally and spatially close to the scene of the accident or its immediate aftermath;

(c) that he suffered shock through sight or hearing of the accident or its immediate aftermath.

In thus following the path taken by Lord Wilberforce in *McLoughlin v. O'Brian* (H.L., 1982) the House of Lords has made it clear that shock cases fall within a distinct category subject to special rules and that reasonable foresight of shock alone is not sufficient to give rise to a duty. With regard to requirement (a) the plaintiff must generally show that he had a relationship of "love and affection" with the primary victim, though this might be presumed in the case of parents and spouses (and, *per* Lord Keith, fiancés) unless there is evidence to the contrary. Less close relations such as brothers and brothers-in-law do not have the benefit of the presumption and must therefore adduce evidence of the closeness of the emotional tie. Despite this general requirement three of their Lordships expressed the view that a bystander might succeed if he witnessed at close hand a particularly horrific catastrophe, provided that a person of reasonable fortitude would be likely to suffer shock but such a possibility was rejected by the Court of Appeal in *McFarlane v. E.E. Caledonia Ltd* (C.A., 1994). Requirements (b) and (c) rule out the possibility of a claim by one who is informed of the event by a third party and who does not come upon the scene of the accident or its immediate aftermath. *Hevican v. Ruane* (H.C., 1991), decided shortly before *Alcock*, must now therefore be regarded as wrongly decided, particularly since the similar case of *Ravenscroft v. Rederiaktiebolaget Transatlantic* (H.C., 1991) was, in the light of *Alcock*, recently reversed by the Court of Appeal. A point directly in issue in *Alcock* was whether a person who witnessed the events of a disaster on television (or radio) could be regarded as sufficiently proximate in time and space. Their Lordships held that, on the facts, such a person could not, because broadcasting guidelines forbade the suffering of identifiable individuals to be televised, and any perception of the actual consequences of the disaster to his relatives came later. In principle, however, Lords Ackner and Oliver thought that there could be circumstances where the simultaneous broadcast of a disaster would be equivalent to direct sight or hearing.

One matter which was not canvassed in *Alcock* was whether a plaintiff could recover for shock caused as a result of witnessing the destruction of property. In *Attia v. British Gas plc* (C.A., 1988) it was held that there was no principle of law that shock in such circumstances could never be regarded as foreseeable. However, since the defendants in that case admitted to owing a duty in respect of the damage to the plaintiff's home, the shock issue was treated as one of remoteness rather than duty, so the question must remain open.

OMISSIONS

As a general rule the defendant does not owe a duty to take positive action to prevent harm to others. Thus, the rescuer who goes to the assistance of others in peril is certainly under no legal obligation to do so. The term "omission" in this context is taken to mean passive inaction, since tortious negligence can invariably be characterised as a failure to take reasonable precautions.

Exceptions to the rule

Most of the cases involving liability for nonfeasance are concerned, directly or indirectly, with the extent to which a defendant is under a duty to prevent harm to the plaintiff caused by the independent act of a third party. It may be the nature of the relationship between the parties which gives rise to the duty, such as employer and employee (*Hudson v. Ridge Manufacturing Co. Ltd* (H.C., 1957), though the duty does not extend to protecting the employee from economic loss; *Reid v. Rush & Tomkins Group plc* (C.A., 1989), or occupier and visitor (see Chap. 8). Alternatively there may be a special relationship between defendant and third party such that there is a positive obligation to control the third party. Examples of such a relationship include gaoler and prisoner (*Home Office v.*

Dorset Yacht Co. Ltd (H.L., 1970)), parent and child (*Carmarthenshire County Council v. Lewis* (H.L., 1955)) and employer and employee (*Hudson v. Ridge Manufacturing Co. Ltd* (H.C., 1957)). Liability might also arise where the defendant negligently causes or permits to be created a source of danger, and it is reasonably foreseeable that third parties may interfere with it and thereby cause damage (as in *Haynes v. Harwood* (C.A., 1935)); or where he fails to abate a known risk created by third parties upon his property (*Sedleigh-Denfield v. O'Callaghan* (H.L., 1940); see Chap. 11).

Where the wilful wrongdoing of a third party causes damage then, in the absence of any of the exceptional cases referred to above, it is very unlikely that the defendant will be liable. Thus, in *P. Perl (Exporters) Ltd v. Camden London Borough Council* (C.A., 1983) the defendants were held not to owe a duty to make their premises secure in order to prevent thieves from breaking in thereby gaining access to, and stealing from, neighbouring occupiers. This issue was further considered by the House of Lords in *Smith v. Littlewoods Organisation Ltd* (H.L., 1987) where the defendants bought a disused cinema with the intention of demolishing it to make way for a supermarket. While the premises were empty vandals gained access and attempts were made to start a fire, though neither the defendants nor the police knew of this. A fire was eventually started which spread and caused damage to adjacent property belonging to the plaintiffs, whose claim was unanimously rejected. Lord Goff said that there was no general duty of care to prevent a third party from causing damage to the plaintiff by deliberate wrongdoing, however foreseeable such harm might be, because the common law does not normally impose liability for pure omissions. His Lordship concluded that none of the exceptional circumstances which might give rise to a duty applied and, since the defendants were unaware of the presence of the vandals, the risk was therefore not foreseeable. Lords Brandon and Griffiths said that the duty owed by the defendants was to take reasonable care to ensure that the cinema was not, and did not become, a source of danger to neighbouring occupiers, but since there was nothing inherently dangerous on the premises, and because the defendants did not know of the vandals' activities, the risk was unforeseeable. Lord Mackay, too, adopted the test of reasonable foresight, but indicated that there might be circumstances where the risk would have to be "highly likely" before it could be regarded as reasonably foreseeable; in this case, he said, whilst it was probable that persons might attempt to enter the vacant premises, it was by no means a probable consequence of the vacation of those premises that they would be set on fire.

Cases of this nature would now presumably be decided on the ground that there would not be a sufficient relationship of proximity between the parties as to make it just and reasonable to impose a duty, rather than simply by applying a test of reasonable foreseeability.

LEGAL IMMUNITIES

By contrast with the solicitor-client relationship, no contract exists between a barrister and his client, and this was long thought to be justification for the rule that a barrister could not be liable in negligence to his client. Following *Hedley Byrne* such an argument was no longer tenable, and in *Rondel v. Worsley* (H.L., 1969) the House of Lords (in holding that an advocate, whether barrister or solicitor, did not owe a duty to his client in respect of the way in which a case was conducted in court) sought to justify the immunity principally upon the policy ground that, in order to fulfil his duty to the court and to the administration of justice, the advocate had to be free from the threat of negligence actions by dissatisfied clients. In *Saif Ali v. Sydney Mitchell & Co. Ltd* (H.L., 1980) the immunity was extended to encompass pre-trial work which is so intimately connected with the conduct of the cause in court that it can fairly be said to be a preliminary decision affecting the way that the cause is to be conducted at the hearing. In *Somasundaram v. M. Julius Melchior & Co.* (C.A., 1989) the view was taken that advice as to a plea in a criminal case fell within the immunity, but that, as regards solicitors, such immunity protected them only *qua* advocates and not where counsel was engaged (but see section 62(1) of the Courts and Legal Services Act 1990). The precise scope of the immunity is unclear, but it extends to claims against an advocate by opposing parties in civil litigation (*Orchard v. South Eastern Electricity Board* (H.C., 1987)) although, on the rather exceptional facts of *Al-Kandari v. J.R. Brown & Co.* (C.A., 1988), it did not protect a solicitor who stepped outside his role as representative simply for his client and who also assumed responsibilities towards his client's opponent. A further policy argument advanced in *Rondel v. Worsley* in support of the immunity was that an action against the advocate would involve a retrial of the issues which arose in the original case, but this would, according to *Hunter v. Chief Constable of West Midlands Police* (H.L., 1981), now appear to operate as an independent bar. Thus, in *Somasundaram* it was held that, even if the advocate was not immune within the *Saif Ali* principle, he still could not be sued if those proceedings would amount to impugning, either directly

or indirectly, a decision on the merits by a court of competent jurisdiction, since to allow such an action would be an abuse of process
and contrary to public policy. The same reasoning was applied in
Smith v. Linskills (H.C., 1995), but the principle was held not to
apply in *Walpole v. Partridge & Wilson* (C.A., 1994) where, as a result
of alleged negligence, the plaintiff had not had a proper opportunity of having his case tried on the merits.

Apart from advocates, certain others, including judges, those
exercising a quasi-judicial function, and witnesses, have a wide
immunity from actions in tort, avowedly in recognition of the public
interest in the due administration of justice. So, too, a litigant does
not owe a duty of care to an opponent as to the manner in which
the litigation is conducted, because the safeguards against impro-
priety are to be found in the rules and procedures governing the
conduct of litigation, and not in tort (*Business Computers International
Ltd v. Registrar of Companies* (H.C., 1987)). For reasons of policy
which are similar to the above, the police function of conducting
an investigation does not give rise to a duty of care either to an
individual member of the public (*Hill v. Chief Constable of West Yorkshire* (H.L., 1988)) or to the subject of that investigation (*Calveley
v. Chief Constable of the Merseyside Police* (H.L., 1989)); nor does the
Crown Prosecution Service owe a duty of care to those it prosecutes,
save where it assumes by conduct a responsibility to an individual
defendant (*Elguzouli-Daf v. Commissioner of Police of the Metropolis*
(C.A., 1995)).

3. NEGLIGENCE: BREACH OF DUTY

THE REASONABLE MAN

Once it is established that the defendant owed to the particular
plaintiff a duty of care, it must then be proved that the defendant
was in breach of duty. Negligence was defined in *Blyth v. Birmingham
Waterworks Co.* (Ex., 1856) as "the omission to do something which a
reasonable man, guided upon those considerations which ordinarily
regulate the conduct of human affairs, would do, or doing something which a prudent and reasonable man would not do." As a
matter of law, therefore, the standard of care required of the
defendant is that of the hypothetical, reasonable man and, whilst

no man is expected to attain perfection, that standard is objective in the sense that it generally takes no account of the idiosyncrasies of the person whose conduct is in question (*Glasgow Corporation v. Muir* (H.L., 1943)). However, whether the defendant has reached the required standard in any given case is a question of fact, so that previous decisions should not be relied upon as precedents for what constitutes negligence.

The standard of reasonable care is therefore invariable in the sense that the law does not recognise differing degrees of negligence, but it is an infinitely flexible concept enabling the court in any given situation to impose standards ranging from very low to very high. For example, the standard required of a participant in a competitive sport *vis-a-vis* spectators and fellow players may be described as low (see, *e.g. Wooldridge v. Sumner* (C.A., 1963)). Conversely, standards imposed on motorists fall little short of a counsel of perfection, and the Court of Appeal in *Nettleship v. Weston* (C.A., 1971) held that the learner driver must exercise the skill of a reasonably competent, experienced driver. Similarly, in *Roberts v. Ramsbottom* (H.C., 1980) the defendant was held liable for an accident after he had unknowingly suffered a minor stroke which impaired his consciousness. The imposition of such high standards may be justified where the defendant is engaged in a high-risk activity, and there can be little doubt that, in some instances, compulsory liability insurance has influenced the court in fixing the level of care.

THE CONCEPT OF RISK

What is reasonable conduct varies with the particular circumstances, and liability depends ultimately on what the reasonable man would have foreseen, which in turn may depend upon what particular knowledge and experience, if any, is to be attributed to him (*Roe v. Minister of Health* (C.A., 1954)). However, whilst the defendant is not negligent if the consequences of his conduct were unforeseeable, it does not necessarily follow that he will be liable for all foreseeable consequences. In practice the courts evaluate the defendant's behaviour in terms of risk, so that he will be adjudged negligent if he exposes the plaintiff to an unreasonable risk of harm. To this end a number of factors must be weighed in the balance, including the magnitude of the risk, the social utility or desirability (if any) of the activity in question, and the cost and practicability of precautionary measures to minimise or eliminate the risk. In performing this balancing act the court will decide what weight is to be given to each of these factors and will make a value

[handwritten annotation at top: "Did the discovery of the blind significantly alter the risk or the job? or was risk on at the time Bash assumed it newly 2 not 1 needed."]

judgment as to what the reasonable man would have done in the circumstances.

Magnitude of the risk

The degree of care which the law exacts must be commensurate with the risk created. Two factors are involved here, namely the likelihood that harm will be caused and the potential gravity of that harm should the risk materialise. In *Bolton v. Stone* (H.L., 1951) the plaintiff was standing in the road when she was struck by a cricket ball which had been hit out of the defendants' ground. There was evidence that this had happened six times in the preceding 30 years, so the risk was one of which the defendants were aware and which was therefore foreseeable. Nevertheless the defendants were held not liable because the risk was so small that they were justified in not taking further measures to eliminate it.

The relevance of the potential gravity of the consequences is illustrated in *Paris v. Stepney B.C.* (H.L., 1951) where a one-eyed garage worker became totally blind after being struck in the eye by a metal chip which flew from a bolt which he was trying to hammer loose. The defendant employers were held liable for failing to provide him with safety goggles, even though they were justified in not providing such equipment to a person with normal sight. Although the risk was small, the injury to this particular plaintiff was very serious.

The degree of risk to which the plaintiff is exposed will also depend, as is evident from *Paris*, upon any physical abnormality from which he may suffer so that, if such abnormality is or ought to be known to the defendant, that is a factor which must be taken into account. Thus, if a hole is dug in the pavement adequate steps must be taken to prevent blind people from falling into it (*Haley v. London Electricity Board* (H.L., 1965)).

Social utility

The purpose to be served, if sufficiently important or desirable, may justify the assumption of what might otherwise be regarded as an abnormal risk. In *Watt v. Hertfordshire C.C.* (C.A., 1954), for example, a fireman was injured by the movement of a heavy jack whilst travelling in a lorry which was not properly equipped to carry it. The jack was urgently needed to save the life of a woman who had become trapped under a bus, and the defendants were accordingly held to be justified in exposing the plaintiff to that risk. On the other hand, the laudable object of saving human life or limb has its limits and is plainly self-defeating if the danger risked is too great, so that a fire authority has been held negligent where a fire engine passed through a red traffic signal on its way to a fire and caused a collision (*Ward v. L.C.C.* (H.C., 1938)).

Cost of precautions

The risk has to be weighed against the cost and practicability of minimising or overcoming it. In *Latimer v. A.E.C. Ltd* (H.L., 1953) a factory floor became slippery with oil and water after a heavy rainfall caused flooding. Despite taking such steps as they were able, the defendants could not entirely eradicate the danger and the plaintiff slipped and was injured. The defendants were held not liable because the risk was not so great as to require the drastic step of closing the factory until the floor dried out.

CHARACTERISTICS OF THE DEFENDANT

It has already been noted that the legal standard generally takes no account of the personal characteristics of the particular defendant, who cannot therefore be heard to say that he did his incompetent best. Inexperience or lack of intelligence or slow reactions provide no excuse to a charge of negligence. Nor, for that matter, will a defendant be able to avail himself of some lower standard on account of his physical disability. A partially sighted driver owes the same duty as one with normal sight, and the fact that he has a reduced field of vision merely imposes upon him an obligation to proceed with greater caution . The reasonable man is expected to know those things that common experience teaches and, in appropriate cases, he can be expected to anticipate that others may be careless. Two types of defendant, children and those professing a particular skill, require special mention.

Children

As far as children are concerned, there is no defence of minority as such and a child is as responsible for his torts (through his guardian *ad litem*) as a person of full age. Thus, a boy of 16 has been held negligent in the use of an air rifle (*Gorely v. Codd* (H.C., 1967)). But, by analogy with the approach adopted in cases of contributory negligence (see Chap. 5), his age will be relevant in determining whether he is capable of the necessary mental state, and he will, it seems, be judged in accordance with standards of behaviour to be reasonably expected of a child his age. This test was applied in the Australian case of *McHale v. Watson* (1966). Where a young child does cause injury by conduct which in an adult would be classed as negligent then, more often than not, a parent or other responsible person, such as a teacher, will be liable. This is not vicarious liability but a primary liability arising from a failure to exercise proper supervision and control (*Carmarthenshire C.C. v. Lewis* (H.L., 1955)).

Professionals

A person who holds himself out as having a particular skill or profession must attain the standard of the reasonably competent man exercising that skill or profession. The level of skill demanded, however, will vary according to the extent of the risk. For example, the do-it-yourself enthusiast fixing a door handle in his home must reach the standard of a reasonably competent carpenter doing that type of work, but not of a professional working for reward (*Wells v. Cooper* (C.A., 1958)). If, however, the work is of a technical or complex nature, and there is a risk of serious injury should it not be properly done, the defendant may be expected either to employ an expert or to display the same degree of skill.

A member of a profession discharges his duty by conforming to the standards of a reasonably competent member of that profession and inexperience is no excuse. Thus, a doctor must act in accordance with a practice accepted as proper by a body of responsible and skilled medical opinion, and is not negligent merely because there is a body of opinion which would take a contrary view. This was the test laid down in *Bolam v. Friern Barnet Hospital Management Committee* (H.C., 1957), and indeed it has since been held that where there is more than one accepted method of doing things, both or all of which are regarded as proper by a skilled body of opinion, the judge is not entitled to make a finding of negligence on the basis of his preference for one method rather than another (*Maynard v. West Midlands Regional Health Authority* (H.L., 1984)). The duty of the doctor is the same whether the matter be one of treatment, diagnosis or advice (*Sidaway v. Governors of the Bethlem Royal Hospital* (H.L., 1985)). Although the *Bolam* test applies to professions generally, it has on occasions been interpreted, in relation only to the medical profession, to mean that practitioners themselves are the final arbiters in determining standards of professional competence. It is clear, however, that this is not so (see, *e.g. Gold v. Haringey Health Authority* (C.A., 1987)), although the effect of the test is undoubtedly to make proof of professional negligence extremely difficult where the defendant has followed an accepted practice.

An error of judgment by a professional may or may not be negligent, depending upon whether it was such as a reasonably competent practitioner might make (*Whitehouse v. Jordan* (H.L., 1981)). Finally, it is part of the professional's duty to keep abreast of new developments and techniques, as what is reasonably foreseeable may depend upon the state of existing knowledge within that profession at the time. Thus, in *Roe v. Minister of Health* (C.A., 1954) an anaesthetist was not negligent in failing to appreciate the risk of percolation of a preservative through invisible cracks in glass ampoules in which the anaesthetic was stored, because such a danger was not known to exist at the time.

EVIDENCE OF NEGLIGENCE

It is for the plaintiff to prove, on a balance of probabilities, that the defendant was negligent, subject to the proviso that proof that a person stands convicted of an offence is conclusive evidence in civil proceedings that he did commit it unless the contrary is proved (Civil Evidence Act 1968, s.11). The effect of this provision is to shift the burden of proof where the plaintiff proves that the defendant has been convicted of an offence involving conduct complained of as negligent, such as careless driving.

Conformity to general practice is generally regarded as evidence that reasonable care has been taken, but this is not conclusive (*Cavanagh v. Ulster Weaving Co. Ltd* (H.L., 1960)) although as indicated above in the case of professionals who have so conformed, negligence is very difficult to establish. Conversely, failure to conform to approved practice may afford prima facie evidence of negligence, but again it is not conclusive of the matter (*Brown v. Rolls Royce Ltd*. (H.L., 1960)).

In order to discharge the burden of proof the plaintiff must usually prove particular conduct on the part of the defendant which can be regarded as negligent. He will not be able to do so, however, if he does not know how the accident was caused and, in such a case, he may be able to rely on the maxim *res ipsa loquitur* (the thing speaks for itself). This is simply a rule of evidence by which the plaintiff, who is unable to explain how the accident happened, asks the court to make a prima facie finding of negligence which it is then for the defendant to rebut if he can. After a long history of uncertainty on the issue, the Privy Council has now held that there is no shift in the legal burden of proof (*Ng Chun Pui v. Lee Chuen Tat* (P.C., 1988)). There are three conditions necessary for the application of the doctrine according to *Scott v. London and St. Katherine Docks Co.*

(E.C., 1865); there must be an absence of explanation as to how the accident happened, the "thing" which causes the damage must be under the control of the defendant (or someone for whose negligence he is responsible), and the accident must be such as would not ordinarily occur without negligence.

With regard to the first requirement, if the cause of the accident is known the doctrine does not apply because all that need then be done is to decide whether, on the facts, negligence is proved (*Barkway v. South Wales Transport Co. Ltd.* (H.L., 1950)). The operation of the second requirement is illustrated in *Easson v. L.N.E.R.* (C.A., 1944) where it was held that the doors of a long distance express train could not be said to be under the continuous control of the defendants, so that a child who fell out of the train could not rely on the maxim. Control by the defendant depends on the probability of outside interference. If the facts establish that such interference was improbable, the defendant will be regarded as being in control.

Whether the accident is such as would not ordinarily have happened without negligence is to be judged in the light of common experience. Thus the maxim has been applied where a plaintiff went into hospital with two stiff fingers and came out with four stiff fingers (*Cassidy v. Ministry of Health* (C.A., 1951)), to an unexplained and violent skid in a vehicle (*Richley v. Faull* (H.C., 1965)), and on a number of occasions to foreign substances found in consumer products (*Grant v. Australian Knitting Mills Ltd.* (P.C., 1936)). In *Ward v. Tesco Stores Ltd.* (C.A., 1976) it was held to apply where the plaintiff slipped on some yoghurt on a supermarket floor but, in view of the absence of evidence as to how long the yoghurt had been there, the decision seems doubtful.

If the maxim applies (and it need not be specifically pleaded) the defendant may be able to rebut the inference of negligence if he can show how the accident actually occurred, and that explanation is consistent with no negligence on his part, or he may be able to provide a reasonable explanation of how the accident could have happened without negligence, in which case one of the essential conditions for the application of the maxim is not satisfied. It must, however, be a reasonable explanation and not merely a theoretical possibility because, one way or another, the defendant must show that the accident is at least as consistent with his having exercised reasonable care as with negligence, and the burden upon him may be very onerous, particularly where there is a high risk of serious harm (*Henderson v. H. E. Jenkins & Sons* (H.L., 1970)).

Who is the defendant/s

4. NEGLIGENCE: CAUSATION AND REMOTENESS OF DAMAGE

The issues of causation and remoteness are relevant to the law of tort generally but are dealt with in the context of negligence because that is where most of the problems have arisen. Unless the plaintiff can prove that the defendant's tort caused his loss he will fail in his action or, in the case of torts actionable *per se*, will recover only nominal damages. Even if he can prove a sufficient causal connection he will still fail if the defendant's breach is not a cause in law of the damage or, to put the matter another way, if the damage is too remote.

FACTUAL CAUSATION

It must first be established that the breach was *a* cause of the damage, not necessarily the sole or principal cause provided it "materially contributed" to the damage (*Bonnington Castings Ltd v. Wardlaw* (H.L., 1956)). In determining this issue it is usual to employ the "but for" test, the function of which is not to allocate legal responsibility, but merely to eliminate those factors which could not have had any causal effect. "If the damage would not have happened but for a particular fault then that fault is the cause of the damage; if it would have happened just the same, fault or no fault, the fault is not the cause of the damage" (*per* Denning L.J. in *Cork v. Kirby Maclean Ltd.* (C.A., 1952)). In *Barnett v. Chelsea & Kensington Hospital Management Committee* (H.C., 1969) the failure of a casualty officer to examine a patient, who later died of arsenic poisoning, was held not to have been a cause of death because evidence showed that the patient would probably have died in any event. The "but-for" test will not, however, always solve the problem as is apparent where two simultaneous wrongs are done to the plaintiff, each of which would in itself be sufficient to cause the damage. In this case the test leads to the absurd result that neither breach is a cause of the damage, whereas in practice both will be held to have caused it.

Difficulties may also arise where the precise cause of the damage is unknown. In *McGhee v. National Coal Board* (H.L., 1972) the plaintiff contracted dermatitis as a result of exposure to abrasive dust at work. His employers were not at fault for the exposure during the normal course of his work, but were negligent in failing to provide washing facilities with the result that he was caked in dust for longer than necessary as he cycled home. The plaintiff succeeded on the ground that it was sufficient to show that the defendants' breach materially increased the risk of injury, even though medical knowledge at the time was unable to establish the breach as the probable cause. This decision had potentially far-reaching effects, particularly for cases of medical negligence, and an attempt was made at first instance in *Hotson v. East Berkshire Area Health Authority* (H.L., 1987) to extend the principle so as to impose liability in respect of the loss of a chance of recovery. The plaintiff injured his hip in a fall and, as a result of negligent medical diagnosis, suffered a permanent deformity the risk of which would, had proper treatment been given, have been reduced by 25 per cent. The trial judge's decision to award that percentage of the loss was upheld in the Court of Appeal but reversed by the House of Lords on the ground that the plaintiff had not proved his case on a balance of probabilities. Had he been able to do so, their Lordships made it clear that there was no principle of law which would have justified a discount from the full measure of damages, incidentally demonstrating that, ignoring any possibility of contributory negligence, the plaintiff's claim is determined on an "all or nothing" basis. Any suggestion that *McGhee*'s case establishes a new principle was decisively rejected by the House of Lords in *Wilsher v. Essex Area Health Authority* (H.L., 1988), where their Lordships simply said that the court in *McGhee* had properly concluded that the breach of duty had materially contributed to the injury.

The position becomes more complex where successive acts cause damage. In *Baker v. Willoughby* (H.L., 1970) the plaintiff's leg was injured through the defendant's negligence, and some time later, before the trial of the action, he was shot during a robbery in the same leg which then had to be amputated. It was held that the plaintiff's right of recovery was not limited to the loss suffered only before the date of the robbery, but that he was entitled to the damages that he would have received had there been no subsequent injury. By contrast, in *Jobling v. Associated Dairies Ltd* (H.L., 1980) the defendants' negligence caused a reduction in the plaintiff's earning capacity. Three years later, but before trial, the plaintiff was found to be suffering from a complaint, wholly unrelated to the original accident, which totally incapacitated him. The defendants were held liable only for the loss up to the time of the plaintiff's disablement. In *Baker* the later act was tortious whereas in *Jobling* it was a natural event, but the distinction is not very compelling. The decision in the former case is perhaps justifiable on the ground that to have applied the "but for" test in its full rigour would have left the plaintiff under-compensated. For even had the robbers been sued to judgment, they would have been liable only for depriving the plaintiff of an already damaged leg.

REMOTENESS OF DAMAGE

It is not for every consequence of the defendant's wrong that the plaintiff is entitled to compensation. In order to contain the defendant's liability within reasonable bounds a line must be drawn, and those consequences which fall on the far side of that line are said to be too remote or, to put the matter another way, are regarded as not having been caused in law by the defendant's breach of duty.

Competing tests

In *Re Polemis* (C.A., 1921) a ship's cargo of benzine had leaked filling the hold with inflammable vapour. Stevedores unloading the vessel negligently dropped a plank into the hold, and the defendant employers were held liable for the destruction of the ship in the ensuing blaze because that loss was a direct, albeit unforeseeable, consequence of the negligence. Whilst not denying the relevance of foreseeability to the existence of a duty, the case did decide that it was not relevant in determining for what consequences the defendant should pay.

This approach was, however, disapproved by the Privy Council in *The Wagon Mound* (P.C., 1961), which substituted a test of reasonable foresight of consequence for that of directness. The defendants negligently discharged into Sydney Harbour a large quantity of fuel oil which drifted to the plaintiffs' wharf where welding was in progress. The plaintiffs discontinued their operations, but later resumed following an assurance that the oil was in no danger of igniting. A fire did eventually break out, however, causing damage to the plaintiffs' wharf and to two ships upon which work was being done. It was found as a fact that some damage to the wharf was reasonably foreseeable by way of fouling of the slipway but that, in view of expert evidence, it was unforeseeable that the oil would ignite. The defendants were accordingly held not liable.

A number of points may be noted here. First, the courts have come to accept *The Wagon Mound* as representing the law. Secondly, the foreseeability of an event and the likelihood or otherwise of its occurring are quite different matters, and whilst the latter may be relevant to the issue of breach of duty (see Chap. 3), the degree

of foresight is generally irrelevant to the question of remoteness
(see, however, the section in this Chapter on intervening acts).
Thus, in *The Wagon Mound (No. 2)* (P.C., 1967) an action brought
by the owners of the vessels damaged in the fire succeeded because
it was found as a fact, on different evidence, that although the
risk of fire was very slight, it was nonetheless foreseeable. Thirdly,
although *The Wagon Mound (No. 2)* held that foreseeability was the
test for remoteness in cases of nuisance also it is unclear how far,
if at all, the principle applies to other torts. It would appear not
to apply where the defendant intends to cause injury because that
"disposes of any question of remoteness", *Quinn v. Leathem* (H.L.,
1901)), but whether torts of strict liability are governed by foreseeability is a matter of controversy. Finally, the general tendency
is to adopt a liberal approach to foreseeability, so that neither the
extent of the harm nor the precise manner of its infliction need
be foreseeable, provided it falls broadly within a foreseeable class
of damage. Taken in conjunction with the "egg-shell skull" principle, this means that, in practice, the same result would often be
achieved whichever of the competing tests is applied.

Manner of occurrence

In *Hughes v. Lord Advocate* (H.L., 1963) post office employees negligently left a manhole uncovered with a canvas shelter over it, sur-
rounded by paraffin lamps. The plaintiff, aged eight, took one of
the lamps into the shelter and knocked it into the manhole. By an
unusual combination of circumstances there was a violent explosion
in which the boy was badly burned. Although the explosion was
unforeseeable, the defendants were held liable because burns from
the lamp were foreseeable, and it was immaterial that the precise
chain of events leading to the injury was not. By way of contrast, in
Doughty v. Turner Manufacturing Co. Ltd (C.A., 1964) the defendants'
employee dropped an asbestos cover into a vat of molten liquid
which, due to an unforeseeable chemical reaction, erupted and
burned a fellow worker standing nearby. It was held that, even if
injury by splashing were foreseeable (which was doubted), the erup-
tion was not, and the plaintiff failed. This case is clearly at odds
with *Hughes*, because if it is accepted that some injury by burning
was foreseeable, then it ought not to matter that the way in which
it occurred was not. On the balance of authority *Hughes* is to be
preferred.

Type of damage

The precise nature of the damage need not be foreseeable, provided it is of a type which could have been foreseen. The difficulty

in defining damage "of a type" is illustrated by two contrasting cases. in *Bradford v. Robinson Rentals Ltd* (H.C., 1967) a van driver sent on a long journey in an unheated vehicle in severe weather was able to recover for frostbite because, although not in itself foreseeable, it was within the broad class of foreseeable risk arising from exposure to extreme cold. In *Tremain v. Pike* (H.C., 1969) the defendant's alleged negligence caused his farm to become rat-infested with the result that the plaintiff contracted a rare disease by contact with rat's urine. It was held that, even if negligence had been proved, the plaintiff could not succeed because although injury from rat bites or food contamination was foreseeable, this particularly rare disease was entirely different in kind. The decision in *Bradford* is a more accurate reflection of the current tendency to adopt a liberal approach to this issue.

Extent of damage; the "egg-shell skull" rule

Subject to what has been said above, it matters not that the actual damage is far greater in extent than could have been foreseen. Thus, in *Vacwell Engineering Co. Ltd v. B.D.H. Chemicals Ltd* (C.A., 1971) the plaintiffs purchased a chemical manufactured and sup-plied by the defendants, who failed to give warning that it was liable to cause a minor explosion upon contact with water. The plaintiffs' employee placed a large quantity of the chemical in a sink whereupon an explosion of unforeseeable violence extensively damaged the premises. Since the explosion and consequent damage were foreseeable, even though the magnitude and extent thereof were not, the defendants were held liable.

A similar rule operates where the plaintiff suffers foreseeable personal injury which is exacerbated by some pre-existing physical or psychic abnormality. This so-called "egg-shell skull" principle survives *The Wagon Mound* (P.C., 1961) and imposes liability upon the defendant for harm which is not only greater in extent than, but which is of an entirely different kind to, that which is foresee-able. In *Smith v. Leech Brain & Co. Ltd* (H.C., 1962) a workman who had a predisposition to cancer received a burn on the lip from molten metal due to a colleague's negligence. The defendants were held liable for his eventual death from cancer triggered off by the burn. The principle applies equally to a plaintiff who suffers from nervous shock (*Brice v. Brown* (H.C., 1984)) and to one with an "egg-shell personality" (*Malcolm v. Broadhurst* (H.C., 1970)). Thus, in *Meah v. McCreamer* (H.C., 1985) the plaintiff underwent a marked personality change brought about by injuries received in a collision for which the defendant was responsible. This led him to commit

a number of serious assaults culminating in a life sentence, and he
recovered damages for the deprivation of his liberty. In *Robinson v.
Post Office* (C.A., 1974) the principle was applied to a plaintiff who
suffered serious damage due to an allergy to medical treatment,
which was foreseeably required as a result of an injury caused by
the defendants' negligence.

According to *Liesbosch Dredger v. S.S. Edison* (H.L., 1933) the "egg-
shell skull" rule does not apply where the plaintiff's loss is aggravated by his own lack of financial resources. The distinction between
physical or psychic peculiarities on the one hand, and lack of means
on the other, appears to have no basis in logic and may be a matter
of policy. Nor is it clear where the line is to be drawn between *The
Liesbosch* and the plaintiff's duty to mitigate his loss. In the latter
case the plaintiff's impecuniosity may be a relevant factor in determining whether he has acted reasonably (*Dodd Properties (Kent) Ltd
v. Canterbury City Council* (C.A., 1980)), and it is worth noting that
whilst the burden rests upon the plaintiff to show that his loss is
not too remote, it is upon the defendant to show that the plaintiff
failed to act reasonably in mitigation. There have been attacks
upon *The Liesbosch* but, notwithstanding attempts to circumvent it,
it is still applied (see, *e.g. Ramwade Ltd v. J. W. Emson & Co. Ltd*
(C.A., 1987)). In *Dodd Properties* the plaintiffs were able to convince
the court that their delay in effecting repairs to their negligently-
damaged property was based upon sound commercial sense rather
than a lack of resources, and it was therefore held that they were
entitled to the higher cost of repairs at the date of trial. Indeed it
is arguable that the rule ought never to apply in the case of damage
to non-profit-earning property so long as liability remains in dis-
pute (see *Perry v. Sidney Phillips & Son* (C.A., 1982)). In *Mattocks v.
Mann* (C.A., 1993) insurers delayed in settling the cost of repair to
the plaintiff's vehicle. The plaintiff, who could not afford to pay
for the repairs herself, was held entitled to the cost of hiring a
replacement during the delay, since it was clearly contemplated
that, in cases of substantial damage, the parties would look to
insurers to meet the cost. It is clear that the uncertainty as to the
precise status of *The Liesbosch* is in urgent need of resolution by the
House of Lords.

INTERVENING CAUSES

In some cases the plaintiff's damage is alleged to be attributable
not to the defendant's breach of duty, but to some intervening
event which breaks the chain of causation. Such an event is called

a *novus actus interveniens* and is usually dealt with as part of the issue of remoteness because even though the damage would not have occurred "but for" the defendant's breach, it may still be regarded in law as falling outside the scope of the risk created by the original fault.

Plaintiff's intervention

In *McKew v. Holland & Hannen & Cubitts (Scotland) Ltd* (H.L., 1969) the plaintiff's leg would give way without warning as a result of an injury caused by the defendants' negligence. Whilst descending a steep flight of steps without assistance or support, his leg gave way and he fell and fractured his ankle. The defendants were held not liable for this further injury because, although foreseeable, the plaintiff's conduct was so unreasonable as to amount to a *novus actus*. In *Sayers v. Harlow U.D.C.* (C.A., 1958) a faulty lock on the door of a public lavatory cubicle caused the plaintiff to become trapped inside. She fell and injured herself when the toilet-roll holder onto which she had climbed in order to get out gave way, and damages were reduced under the Law Reform (Contributory Negligence) Act 1945 (see Chap. 5) for the unreasonable manner in which she had attempted her escape.

These two cases illustrate the different approach that may be taken where the damage is caused by a combination of the plaintiff's own act and the defendant's breach. Whether the issue is seen as one of *novus actus* or of contributory negligence (which is the more common approach) will depend upon the nature and quality of the plaintiff's conduct, and it may be that a positive act is more likely to break the causal chain than a mere omission (*cf. Knightley v. Johns* (C.A., 1982); see below). On any view of the matter *McKew* seems to be a harsh decision. There may be instances where even a deliberate act by the plaintiff will not relieve the defendant of responsibility. Thus, in *Pigney v. Pointer's Transport Services Ltd* (H.C., 1957) the defendants were held liable to a plaintiff whose husband committed suicide as a result of mental depression brought on by an injury caused by the defendants' negligence. In a case such as this it would surely make little sense to stigmatise as unreasonable the conduct of one whose capacity for rational judgment has been impaired by the initial injury. In any event, the decision is presumably justifiable on the basis of the "egg-shell skull" principle. *Meah v. McCreamer* is to similar effect, but in *Meah v. McCreamer (No. 2)* (H.C., 1986) an action by the plaintiff to recover the compensation awarded to the victims of his assaults failed for policy reasons on the ground that to hold the defendant liable would be to impose upon him an indeterminate liability for an indefinite time. The loss was accordingly held to be too remote.

As far as rescuers are concerned (see Chap. 5), there is generally no question of categorising the plaintiff's conduct as a *novus actus* (*Haynes v. Harwood* (C.A., 1935)), unless the danger has passed, in which case it is arguable that a duty is no longer owed (see *Cutler v. United Dairies (London) Ltd* (C.A., 1933)). It makes no difference in principle whether the rescuer acts on impulse or after conscious reflection (*Haynes v. Harwood, per* Greer L.J.).

Intervention of third party

According to Lord Reid in *Dorset Yacht Co. Ltd v. Home Office* (H.L., 1970) the intervention of a third party must have been something *very likely* to happen if it is not to be regarded as breaking the chain of causation. However, this *dictum* should be interpreted in the light of its proper context, namely the potential liability of a defendant for the criminal act of another, because a less stringent test may be applied in the case of non-wilful intervention by the third party. In *Knightley v. Johns* (C.A., 1982) the defendant negligently caused a crash on a dangerous bend in a one-way tunnel. The police inspector at the scene of the accident forgot to close the tunnel to oncoming traffic as he ought to have done in accordance with standing orders, so he ordered the plaintiff officer to ride back on his motorcycle against the flow of traffic in order to do so, and the plaintiff was injured in a further collision. It was said that, in considering whether the intervening act of a third party breaks the chain of causation, the test is whether the damage is reasonably foreseeable in the sense of being a "natural and probable" result of the defendant's breach. A deliberate decision to do a positive act is more likely to break the chain than a mere omission; so too, tortious conduct is more likely to break it than conduct which is not. In this case the inspector's errors amounted to tortious negligence which could scarcely be described as the natural and probable consequence of the original collision, and the defendant was therefore not liable. It must be decided in each case whether the nature of the intervening actor's conduct was such as to eclipse the causative effect of the original wrong. In *Rouse v. Squires* (C.A., 1973) the negligence of the first defendant in causing a motorway crash was held to be an operative cause of the death of the plaintiff who, whilst assisting at the scene of the accident, was run down by the negligent driving of the second defendant. By contrast, in *Wright v. Lodge* (C.A., 1993) the defendant's negligence caused a lorry driver to collide with his car, as a result of which the lorry was involved in a further collision. It was found that the lorry driver had driven recklessly (not merely carelessly), and his driving was therefore held to be the sole legal cause of the damage arising from the second accident.

A question which as yet remains unresolved is the extent to which negligent medical treatment or diagnosis may break the chain of causation, although the answer will no doubt depend upon the extent to which the practitioner has departed from the requisite standard of care. In *Prendergast v. Sam & Dee Ltd* (H.C., 1988) the negligent misreading by a pharmacist of a doctor's prescription did not relieve the doctor of his duty to write in a reasonably legible hand, and liability was apportioned between them.

The problems which arise in those cases involving wilful wrongdoing by third parties may be analysed either in terms of duty or of remoteness. The former analysis is more usual where the only damage suffered is that caused by the intervening actor (*e.g.* the *Dorset Yacht* case), and if a duty to prevent such damage is held to exist, it follows that, assuming a breach of the duty, the damage cannot be too remote (see Chap. 2 for a fuller discussion). Where, however, the defendant's breach causes some initial damage and thereby affords an opportunity for further damage to be done by the third party, the courts tend to view the issue as one of remoteness. Thus, in *Lamb v. Camden London Borough Council* (C.A., 1981) a local authority whose servants negligently damaged the foundations of the plaintiff's house was held not liable for subsequent damage done by squatters who moved in while the house was unoccupied. The Court of Appeal thought that Lord Reid's observation in the *Dorset Yacht* case understated the degree of likelihood required, and, according to Oliver L.J., there may be circumstances where the third party's act must be virtually inevitable before the defendant can be held liable (see, *e.g. Ward v. Cannock Chase District Council* (H.C., 1986)).

In dealing generally with the question of what amounts to a *novus actus*, the answer is sometimes to be found by considering whether the intervening conduct was within the ambit of the risk created by the defendant's negligence. Thus, an incursion of squatters is not one of the risks attendant upon undermining the foundations of a building (*Lamb*'s case); but the act of a rescuer who goes to assist another put in peril by the defendant's negligence clearly is within the risk created by that negligence and is not therefore a *novus actus* (*Haynes v. Harwood* (C.A., 1935); see Chap. 5).

Intervening natural force

The defendant will not normally be liable for damage suffered as the immediate consequence of a natural event which occurs independently of the breach. In *Carslogie Steamship Co. Ltd v. Royal Norwegian Government* (H.L., 1952) the defendants were held not liable for storm damage suffered by a ship during a voyage to a place where repairs to collision damage caused by the defendants' negligence were to be done, even though that voyage would not have been undertaken had the collision not occurred.

It will be apparent from the foregoing discussion that, in the case of intervening acts, foreseeability may be a rough guide in assessing relative degrees of responsibility but it can never be the sole criterion of liability. A number of the cases evince a notable lack of consistency of approach and precision in the use of language, which serves only to mask the policy factors at play in the judicial process.

---

5. CONTRIBUTORY NEGLIGENCE, VOLENTI NON FIT INJURIA AND EX TURPI CAUSA

CONTRIBUTORY NEGLIGENCE

At common law a plaintiff whose injuries were caused partly by his own negligence could recover nothing. To succeed in this defence it is not necessary for the defendant to prove that the plaintiff owed him a duty of care but simply that he "did not in his own interest take reasonable care of himself and contributed, by this want of care, to his own injury" (*per* Lord Simon in *Nance v. British Columbia Electric Ry.* (P.C., 1951)). Since the Law Reform (Contributory Negligence) Act 1945, contributory negligence is no longer a complete bar to recovery but, in accordance with section 1(1) of the Act, will result in a reduction of damages "to such extent as the court thinks just and equitable having regard to the claimant's share in the responsibility for the damage."

The Act applies where the damage is attributable to the fault of both parties, and "fault" is defined in section 4 to mean "negligence, breach of statutory duty or other act or omission which gives rise to a liability in tort or would, apart from this Act, give rise to the defence of contributory negligence." The defence therefore applies to actions other than in negligence, though it does not apply to deceit (*Alliance & Leicester Building Society v. Edgestop Ltd* (H.C., 1994)) or intentional interference with goods (Torts (Interference with Goods) Act 1977, s.11). Where there is a concurrent liability in contract and tort the plaintiff cannot avoid the apportionment provisions of the Act by framing his action in contract alone (*Forsikringsaktieselskapet Vesta v. Butcher* (C.A., 1988)).

Causation

The damage suffered must be caused partly by the fault of the plaintiff and it is therefore irrelevant that his fault was nothing to do with the accident. Thus, reductions have been made for failing to wear a seat belt or a crash helmet, and for travelling in a vehicle with a drunk driver. To put the matter another way the plaintiff's damage must be within the foreseeable risk to which he unreasonably exposed himself. In *Jones v. Livox Quarries Ltd* (C.A., 1952) the plaintiff, contrary to instructions, stood on the rear towbar of a vehicle and was injured when another vehicle ran into the back of it. It was held that this was one of the risks to which he had exposed himself and his damages were reduced accordingly. On the other hand, where an employee fell through a rotten floor in a room housing dangerous machinery which bore a notice forbidding him to enter, no reduction was made because that was not a risk which he could have foreseen (*Westwood v. Post Office* (H.L., 1974)).

Standard of care

The plaintiff is expected to show an objective standard of reasonable care in much the same way as the defendant must to avoid tortious negligence. He is thus guilty of contributory negligence if he ought reasonably to have foreseen that, if he did not act as a reasonable man, he might be hurt himself. Similar factors to those determining whether the defendant is in breach of duty (see Chap. 3) are therefore relevant here.

Particular cases

1. Children

As a matter of law there is no age below which it can be said that a child is incapable of contributory negligence, but the degree of care to be expected must be proportioned to the age of the child. In *Gough v. Thorne* (C.A., 1966), for example, a 13-year-old girl who was knocked down by a negligent motorist when she stepped past a stationary lorry whose driver had beckoned her to cross, was held not guilty of contributory negligence. On the other hand, in *Morales v. Eccleston* (C.A., 1991) an 11-year-old who was struck by the defendant driver while kicking a ball in the middle of a road with traffic passing in either direction had his damages reduced by 75 per cent. In *Yachuk v. Oliver Blais Co. Ltd* (P.C., 1949) a boy of nine was not contributorily negligent when he set fire to petrol supplied to him by the defendants, on the ground that it was foreseeable that he might meddle with it and he could not be expected to appreciate its dangerous properties.

2. Old or infirm persons

It seems that some latitude may be given to such persons in assessing whether they are guilty of contributory negligence. Thus, an elderly person who is unable to move quickly enough to get out of the path of a motorist who drives close by in the expectation that he is able to do so may not be penalised (*Daly v. Liverpool Corp.* (H.C., 1939)).

3. Rescuers

It is not often that a rescuer will be found guilty of contributory negligence, bearing in mind that, in the face of imminent danger, his reaction is usually instinctive. Thus, in *Brandon v. Osborne, Garrett & Co. Ltd* (H.C., 1924) the defendants negligently allowed a sheet of glass to fall from their shop roof and the plaintiff, believing her husband to be in danger, tried to pull him away and injured her leg. It was held that she was not contributorily negligent. A similar principle applies where the plaintiff is injured in trying to extricate himself from a perilous situation in which the defendant's negligence has placed him, even though with hindsight he is shown to have chosen the wrong course of action (*Jones v. Boyce* (1816) *cf. Sayers v. Harlow U.D.C.* (C.A., 1958)). That a rescuer may be contributorily negligent, however, is illustrated by *Harrison v. British Railways Board* (H.C., 1981), although in this case the plaintiff was plainly at fault in not following an established work procedure designed to deal with the particular emergency in question.

4. Workmen

In relation to actions for breach of statutory duty, this issue is dealt with in Chap. 9. It seems clear from *Westwood v. Post Office* (H.L., 1974) that the more lenient approach towards workmen is appropriate only where the action is founded upon the employer's breach of statutory duty and not upon ordinary negligence.

5. Car passengers

Froom v. Butcher (C.A., 1976) firmly established that failure to wear a seat belt is contributory negligence, provided of course that such failure causes or contributes to the injury. It was suggested that ordinarily there should be a reduction of 25 per cent. in respect of injuries which would have been avoided altogether, and 15 per cent. in respect of those which would have been less severe. Although these figures are guidelines only they should, according to *Capps v. Miller* (C.A., 1989), generally be followed. So, too, a motor-cyclist who fails to wear a crash helmet will have his damages similarly reduced (*O'Connell v. Jackson* (C.A., 1972)), although failure to fasten a helmet properly has been held to merit a slightly smaller reduction (*Capps v. Miller*). It is also clear that to ride in a car in the knowledge that the driver has been drinking constitutes contributory negligence, even though the passenger himself is so intoxicated as not to appreciate that the driver is unfit to drive (*Owens v. Brimmell* (H.C., 1977)).

Apportionment

Apportionment is on a just and equitable basis according to the 1945 Act and, in assessing the plaintiff's reduction, the court may take into account both the causative potency of his act and the degree of blameworthiness (*i.e.* the extent to which his conduct fell below the requisite standard of care) to be attached to it. There seem to be no hard and fast rules, however, and a good deal of judicial discretion is exercised in the matter. The Court of Appeal has held that no apportionment should be made unless one of the parties is at least 10 per cent. to blame (*Johnson v. Tennant Bros. Ltd* (C.A., 1954)), although the case seems to have been decided on the ground that the defendant's breach was not a cause of the damage (see *Capps v. Miller* (C.A., 1989)). In *Jayes v. IMI (Kynoch) Ltd* (C.A., 1985) the plaintiff was adjudged 100 per cent. contributorily negligent, but such a finding is illogical according to *Pitts v. Hunt* (C.A., 1990) because the 1945 Act does not apply unless both parties were at fault. The earlier case can presumably be explained on the basis that the plaintiff was solely to blame for the damage.

Where the same accident involves two or more defendants, any contributory negligence must be assessed by comparing the plaintiff's conduct with the totality of the defendants' negligence. The issue of the extent to which each defendant contributed to the damage should thereafter be dealt with in contribution proceedings (*Fitzgerald v. Lane* (H.L., 1988)).

One final point to note is that a defendant who seeks to rely on the defence must plead it (*Fookes v. Slaytor* (C.A., 1978)).

VOLENTI NON FIT INJURIA

This maxim embodies the principle that a person who expressly or impliedly agrees with another to run the risk of harm created by that other cannot thereafter sue in respect of damage suffered as a result of the materialisation of that risk. The defence is commonly called consent or voluntary assumption of risk and, if successful, is a complete bar to recovery.

For the defence to apply, the defendant must have committed what would, in the absence of any consent, amount to a tort. The defendant must prove not only that the plaintiff consented to the risk of actual damage, but also that he agreed to waive his right of action in respect of that damage. The application of the defence is most straightforward in the case of intentional torts, as, for instance, where each party to a boxing match consents to being fairly struck by the other. Most of the problems in the past have arisen in negligence where the infliction of damage is a risk rather than a certainty, but in view of the power to apportion responsibility by a finding of contributory negligence, the defence is rarely successful today.

Knowledge of the risk
Mere knowledge of the risk does not amount to consent. It must be found as a fact that the plaintiff freely and voluntarily, with full knowledge of the nature and extent of the risk, impliedly agreed to incur it (*Osborne v. L. & N. W. Ry.* (H.C., 1888)). The plaintiff must therefore have genuine freedom of choice which predicates the absence of any feeling of constraint (*Bowater v. Rowley Regis Corporation* (C.A., 1944)). One explanation for the lack of success of this defence to a negligence action is that, since the alleged consent usually precedes the defendant's breach of duty, the plaintiff cannot be said in these circumstances to have full knowledge and appreciation of the risk (*Wooldridge v. Sumner* (C.A., 1963), *per* Diplock L.J.).

Agreement
It has been suggested that an appreciation of, and willingness to take, the risk will not satisfy the requirements of the defence; there

must, in addition, be evidence that the plaintiff has expressly or impliedly agreed to waive his right of action (see, *e.g. Nettleship v. Weston* (C.A., 1971) *per* Lord Denning). On the other hand the defence may apply where the plaintiff consciously assumes the risk of an existing danger created by the defendant, independently of any agreement (*Titchener v. British Railways Board* (H.L., 1983)).

An express antecedent agreement to relieve the defendant of liability for future negligence operates in effect as an exclusion notice and is therefore subject to the Unfair Contract Terms Act 1977. Section 2(1) renders void any purported exclusion of liability for death or personal injury caused by negligence and, in the case of other loss or damage, section 2(2) subjects such an exclusion to a test of reasonableness. Section 2(3) further provides that a person's agreement to, or awareness of, such a notice is not of itself to be taken as indicating his voluntary acceptance of any risk. It should be noted, however, that these provisions only apply to business liability (see further Chap. 8). In *Johnstone v. Bloomsbury Health Authority* (C.A., 1991) it was considered that, on the assumption that an express contractual term amounted to a plea of violenti, it could fall within the ambit of section 2(1) of the Act.

In some circumstances the conduct of the parties may enable an inference to be drawn that the plaintiff has impliedly agreed to waive his legal rights in respect of future negligence. Thus, in *Morris v. Murray* (C.A., 1990) the defence applied when, in poor weather conditions, the defendant, who to the plaintiff's knowledge was extremely drunk, took the plaintiff for a spin in his aircraft and crashed almost immediately after take-off.

Particular cases

1. Sporting events

A spectator injured by a participant in a sporting event does not consent to negligence either by the participant or by the organiser, though he may be defeated by a valid exclusion notice (*White v. Blackmore* (C.A., 1972)). A spectator may be taken to have accepted those risks ordinarily incidental to the game (*e.g.* being hit by a cricket ball struck into the crowd), but in this case there is no negligence and violenti is therefore irrelevant. The potential liability of the participant depends upon the standard of care owed and, in *Wooldridge v. Sumner* (C.A., 1963), this was expressed by Diplock L.J. as a duty not to act with reckless disregard for the spectator's safety. This was criticised, however, in *Wilks v. Cheltenham Home Guard Motor Cycle & Light Car Club* (C.A., 1971) where it was said that the proper standard was one of reasonable care in all the circumstances, which might include the fact that the defendant is involved in a fast-moving, competitive sport in an all-out effort to win. As between one player and another a similar approach was adopted in *Condon v. Basi* (C.A., 1985) where, however, a "reckless and dangerous" tackle in a local amateur football match was held to be negligent.

2. Workmen

Since *Smith v. Baker & Sons* (H.L., 1891) a plea of *volenti* by an employer in an action by his employee for common law negligence is almost bound to fail, because the unequal nature of the relationship is such that the employee does not exercise complete freedom of will (*Bowater v. Rowley Regis Corporation* (C.A., 1944)). It has further been held that the defence is not available in an action for breach of an employer's statutory duty, though it may succeed where the employer is sued vicariously, provided that the person in breach is not superior in rank to the plaintiff such that his instructions are bound to be obeyed (*I.C.I. Ltd v. Shatwell* (H.L., 1965)). In *Johnstone v. Bloomsbury Health Authority* (C.A., 1991) an express term in a contract of employment required the plaintiff to work 40 hours per week and to "be available" for a further average 48 hours per week overtime at the employer's discretion. In an action for breach of the employer's common law duty to take reasonable care for the plaintiff's health and safety, Leggatt L.J. took the view that the express term could not be overridden by the implied duty, and Browne-Wilkinson V.-C. would have agreed if the term had imposed an absolute obligation to work those further hours, as opposed to giving a discretion. If this view is correct it would appear to undermine the proposition that *volenti* ought not, in principle, to afford a defence to the employer.

3. Car passengers

A passenger who accepts a lift with a driver who, to his knowledge, is inexperienced or whose ability to drive safely is otherwise impaired (*e.g.* through drink) cannot be held *volenti* to the risk, because section 149 of the Road Traffic Act 1988 prohibits any restriction on the driver's liability to his passenger as is required to be covered by insurance (*Pitts v. Hunt* (C.A., 1990); *c.f.* travelling in a plane with a drunken pilot as in *Morris v. Murray* (C.A., 1990)). Taking a lift with an inebriated car driver is, however, likely to amount to contributory negligence (*Owens v. Brimmell* (H.C., 1977)).

4. Rescuers

If the defendant, by his negligence, endangers the safety of others such that a rescue attempt is reasonably foreseeable, he owes a duty to the rescuer (*Haynes v. Harwood* (C.A., 1935)). It makes no difference that the person imperilled is the defendant himself rather than a third party (*Harrison v. British Railways Board* (H.C., 1981)), and the duty owed is wholly independent of any duty owed by the defendant to those who are rescued (*Videan v. British Transport Commission* (C.A., 1963)). Nor is there any rule of law to prevent a claim by a professional "rescuer", so that a fireman injured whilst fighting a negligently-started fire may recover (*Ogwo v. Taylor* (H.L., 1988)). In these situations *volenti* clearly does not apply. In the first place the rescuer acts under moral compulsion and does not therefore exercise freedom of choice, and secondly, since the defendant's negligence precedes the rescue the plaintiff cannot be said to consent to it and may not even be aware of it at the time (*Baker v. T. E. Hopkins & Son Ltd* (C.A., 1959)). In *Chadwick v. British Transport Commission* (H.C., 1967) a rescuer who assisted at the scene of a train crash and who suffered nervous shock as a result of what he saw was held entitled to recover, even though he was in no personal danger. However, it is not necessarily sufficient, particularly in the case of a professional, simply to describe what the plaintiff was doing as "rescue" so as to entitle him to an automatic right of recovery for psychiatric damage. The nature and extent of the plaintiff's involvement must be such as to make it fair and reasonable that the plaintiff should recover when a passive bystander would not (*Frost v. Chief Constable of South Yorkshire* (H.C., 1995)). This has nothing to do with the doctrine of *volenti* as such, but rather with the circumstances in which a duty will be owed to the rescuer (see also Chap. 2). These principles apply equally to the rescue of property (*Hyett v. Great Western Ry.* (C.A., 1948)) although it is unlikely that a person would be justified in taking the same risks.

EX TURPI CAUSA

If the alleged wrong occurs while the plaintiff is engaged in criminal activity his claim may be barred because *ex turpi causa non oritur actio* (no action can be founded on an illegal act). This principle is based upon public policy and may also apply where the plaintiff's conduct is immoral (*Kirkham v. Chief Constable of Greater Manchester* (C.A., 1990)). The difficulty is in determining which types of conduct are considered sufficiently heinous for the purposes of the defence. Some cases have said that it will apply where it would be impossible to determine an appropriate standard of care (*e.g. Pitts v. Hunt* (C.A., 1990)), while others have suggested that the plaintiff ought not to succeed if to permit him to do so would be an "affront to the public conscience" (*Kirkham v. Chief Constable of Greater Manchester*).

Both the degree of moral turpitude and the closeness of the causal connection between it and the plaintiff's damage are relevant factors. Thus, the principle was applied to a plaintiff car passenger injured by the defendant's negligent driving during the course of making their get-away from a burglary (*Ashton v. Turner* (H.C., 1981)); and to one who, having had a few drinks with the defendant, then rode as a pillion passenger on the defendant's motorcycle and encouraged him to drive in a reckless manner, in the knowledge also that the defendant did not hold a licence and was uninsured (*Pitts v. Hunt* (C.A., 1990)). In *Kirkham* (above) the defence was held not to apply to a claim based directly on the suicide of a man who was mentally disturbed, though it was considered that the position might be otherwise where the suicide was entirely sane; the same conclusions were reached in relation to the application of the *volenti* defence.

According to Lord Denning a burglar bitten by a guard dog may be defeated by the maxim (*Cummings v. Granger* (C.A., 1977)), as may one who instigates an affray and gets "more than he bargained for" (*Murphy v. Culhane* (C.A., 1977)). In *Rance v. Mid-Downs Health Authority* (H.C., 1991) the plaintiff alleged that the defendants negligently failed to detect a foetal abnormality during pregnancy and to advise her of her right to terminate it, with the result that she gave birth to a seriously handicapped child. It was held that even if the defendants were negligent, they could not be liable because the pregnancy was so far advanced by the time of the alleged negligence that, as the law then stood, abortion would have been a criminal offence.

---

6. LIABILITY FOR DANGEROUS PRODUCTS

Part I of the Consumer Protection Act 1987, which came into force on March 1, 1988 was enacted to give effect to an EC Directive of 1985, requiring the harmonisation of law on product liability throughout the Community. Subject to certain defences, the Act creates a regime of strict liability, although existing common law rights remain unaffected so that if, for some reason, the Act does not apply a plaintiff may still be able to sue in negligence.

STRICT LIABILITY UNDER THE 1987 ACT

Although a successful claim under the Act is not dependent upon proof of negligence, the plaintiff will have to prove that he suffered damage caused wholly or partly by a defect in a product.

Parties to the action and the meaning of "product"

No mention is made in the Act of who may be able to sue, so anyone who suffers damage would appear to be covered, whether a user of the product in question or not. As far as potential defendants are concerned, section 2(2) provides that the following are liable for the damage:

(a) the producer of the product;

(b) any person who holds himself out as producer by putting his name or trade mark or other distinguishing mark on the product;

(c) an importer of the product into a Member State from a place outside the EC in order to supply it to another in the course of his business.

The term "producer" is defined in section 1(2) to mean either the manufacturer, or the person who won or abstracted the product (*e.g.* as in the case of mineral deposits) or, where the product has not been manufactured, won or abstracted but the essential characteristics of which are attributable to an industrial or other process having been carried out, the person who carried out that process. Furthermore, by section 2(3), the mere supplier (*e.g.* retailer) is liable if he fails within a reasonable time to comply with the plaintiff's request to identify one or more of the persons to whom section 2(2) (see above) applies, or to identify his own supplier.

"Product" is defined in section 1(2) as any goods or electricity and, although the definition of "goods" in a later part of the Act is wide enough to cover fixtures in buildings and component parts of the building itself, there is no liability where goods are supplied by virtue of the creation or disposal of an interest in land. Component parts and raw materials also fall within the definition of "product" as distinct from the overall product in which they are comprised. Thus, where X manufactures a product containing a defective component manufactured by Y which causes damage (*e.g.* a car with faulty brakes), both X and Y are jointly and severally liable. However, section 1(3) in effect provides that the mere supplier of a product containing component parts will not, by reason only of that supply, be treated as supplying those components. This means that liability under section 2(3) in respect of a product containing a defective component will only arise for failure to identify the producer or supplier of the finished product.

It has been noted that, where the essential characteristics of a product are attributable to an industrial or other process having been carried out, the processor may be liable as a producer within the meaning of section 1(2). The failure of the legislature to define "essential characteristics" or "industrial or other process" may present difficulties of interpretation, particularly with regard to foodstuffs. The potential problems are high-lighted by section 2(4), which provides that no person shall be liable "in respect of any defect in any game or agricultural produce if the only supply of the game or produce by that person to another was at a time when it had not undergone an industrial process." In other words, farmers and other suppliers of agricultural produce (defined in section 1(2) as "any produce of the soil, of stock-farming or of fisheries") will be exempt from liability unless, at the time of their supply of it to another, it can be said to have been through an industrial process. If it has, any person to whom section 2(2) or 2(3) applies will be liable, though the liability of the processor as producer in accordance with section 1(2) is dependent upon the essential characteristics of the product being attributable to the industrial process. It is irrelevant, however, that the defect was not in any way caused by that process.

The meaning of "defect"

According to section 3(1) a product is defective if its safety is not such as persons generally are entitled to expect. The "safety" of a product expressly includes safety "with respect to products comprised in that product" (*i.e.* components and raw materials), and a product may be unsafe not only if there is a risk of personal injury but also if it poses a risk of damage to property. In determining what persons generally are entitled to expect, section 3(2) provides that account shall be taken of all the circumstances including the following specific matters:

(a) the way in which and the purposes for which the product has been marketed, its get-up, and warnings and instructions for use accompanying it:

(b) what might reasonably be expected to be done with or in relation to the product:

(c) the time when the product was supplied by its producer to another.

The reference in (a) to the purposes for which the product has been marketed may indicate that a balance has to be struck between known risks associated with a product and the benefits which it seeks to confer. Adopting this interpretation in the case of drugs, for example, a product which produces harmful side-effects is not necessarily defective if its disadvantages are outweighed by the long-term benefits. With regard to (b), a product which is clearly intended for a particular use may not be defective if it causes damage when put to an entirely different use. Similarly, where the defendant reasonably contemplates that something would be done to the product before use (*e.g.* testing), he may argue that there is no defect if that thing is not done (*cf Kubach v. Hollands* (H. C., 1937); *Grant v. Australian Knitting Mills Ltd.* (P.C., 1936)). The provision of appropriate warnings and instructions may clearly be relevant here, and there would therefore appear to be some overlap with (a) in this respect. As far as (c) is concerned, it should be noted that it is the time of supply by the producer to another which is relevant, not the time of supply to the consumer. The concluding words of section 3(2) provide that the mere fact that a product supplied after that time is safer than the product in question does not require the inference that there is a defect. This clearly makes allowance for the fact that improved safety standards are constantly being developed, so that what is considered safe, say, in 1990, will not necessarily be so in 1995.

Damage

Section 5(1) defines damage for the purposes of Part I as death or personal injury, or loss of or damage to property (including land). Claims for property damage are, however, limited in several important respects. First, the defendant will not be liable for damage to the defective product itself, nor for damage to any product supplied with a defective component comprised in it (section 5(2)). A parallel may be drawn here with the common law, where such claims are regarded as being concerned essentially with the quality of the product so that, in the absence of a contract, there is generally no liability in tort on the ground that the loss is purely economic (*Muirhead v. Industrial Tank Specialities Ltd.* (C.A., 1986); see Chap. 2). Secondly, there is no liability unless, at the time of the damage, the property was "of a description of property ordinarily intended for private use, occupation or consumption" and was intended by the plaintiff mainly for such purposes (section 5(3)). A person who suffers damage to his business property must therefore sue in negligence. Finally, no claim will lie where its value does not exceed £275, excluding interest (section 5(4)).

Defences

Section 4(1), paragraphs (a) to (f), provides for the following defences:

(a) The defect is attributable to compliance either with a domestic enactment or with Community law.

(b) The defendant did not at any time supply the product to another. A broad definition is given to "supply" in a later Part of the Act to include not only the usual types of supply contract, but also gifts.

(c) The defendant supplied the product otherwise than in the course of his business *and* either he does not fall within section 2(2) (*i.e.* he is not a producer, "own-brander" or importer) or he does so only by virtue of things done otherwise than with a view to profit. Thus, for example, the producer of home-made wine who gives a bottle to a friend (or, indeed, who charges simply to cover the costs of his production) will be protected.

(d) The defect did not exist at the relevant time. By section 4(2) the "relevant time" means, in relation to electricity, the time at which it was generated; as far as all other products are concerned it means, in the case of the defendant to whom section 2(2) applies, the time when he supplied the product to another and, in the case of a supplier, the time of the last supply by a person who is within the ambit of that section.

(e) The state of scientific and technical knowledge at the relevant time was not such that a producer of products of the same description as the product in question might be expected to have discovered the defect if it had existed in his products while they were under his control. This is the so-called "development risks" or "state of the art" defence which has provoked considerable controversy, not least because it would appear to offer a wider protection than the corresponding provision of the Directive which it seeks to implement. Whereas Article 7 of the Directive would only allow the defence if the state of scientific and technical knowledge was not such as to *enable* the existence of the defect to be discovered, section 4(1) (*e*) of the Act talks in terms of what *might be expected* to have been discovered by a producer of products of the same description as the product in question. The statutory language may thus lead to the inference that the defendant is to be judged by the standards of the hypothetical, reasonable producer of the same, or similar, products, which is tantamount to saying that the defendant will not be liable in the absence of negligence. It must be remembered, however, that the onus is upon the defendant to establish the defence. "Relevant time" bears the same meaning as in (d) above and will normally be the time of supply of the product by a person to whom section 2(2) applies.

(f) The defect constituted a defect in a product containing the defendant's component part (or raw material) and was wholly attributable to the design of the overall product or to compliance by the defendant with instructions given by the producer of the overall product.

Apart from the above defences, the effect of section 6(4) is to preserve the plaintiff's contributory negligence as a partial defence to a claim against any person under the Act.

Miscellaneous

It has been noted that the plaintiff must prove that the damage was caused wholly or partly by the defect. It seems clear that there can be no question of categorising the damage as too remote but if, for example, the plaintiff seriously misuses the product, or an intermediary fails to follow clear instructions (*e.g.* to test before use), it is unlikely that the product would be found to be defective. Once it has been categorised as defective, however, failure by an intermediary to examine it will not defeat the action on grounds of causation.

Three final points are worthy of note. First, although there is a limitation period of three years, this is subject to an overall long-stop period of 10 years from the relevant time (see above), after which no claim may be brought. Thus, for example, where a product manufactured and distributed in 1987 causes damage in 1998, a claim against the manufacturer will lie only in negligence. Secondly, section 7 of the Act prevents the defendant from limiting or excluding his liability, either contractually or otherwise. Thirdly, section 1(1) states that the purpose of Part I of the Act is to give effect to the Directive and that it should be construed accordingly. Any ambiguity in the Act should therefore be resolved, wherever possible, by reference to the Directive and not merely in accordance with traditional canons of construction.

COMMON LAW NEGLIGENCE

Where the Consumer Protection Act does not apply, the plaintiff must rely upon his existing common law remedies. If he acquires defective goods under a sale or similar supply contract his first line of attack is to sue the supplier for breach of implied undertakings relating to quality. Although these contractual obligations are generally imposed only upon those who supply in the course of a business, they are strict and entitle the plaintiff to recover both in respect of goods which simply fail to work or which are less valuable than those contracted for, and where the defect causes personal injury or damage to property. If the plaintiff does not have a contract, however, or indeed where an action against his supplier is not viable (*e.g.* the supplier is in liquidation), he may pursue an action in tort.

The manufacturer's duty

The source of the duty owed by a manufacturer to the ultimate consumer is to be found in the so-called narrow rule in *Donoghue v. Stevenson* (H.L., 1932), expressed by Lord Atkin as follows:

> "A manufacturer of products, which he sells in such a form as to show that he intends them to reach the ultimate consumer in the form in which they left him with no reasonable possibility of intermediate examination, and with the knowledge that the absence of reasonable care in the preparation or putting up of the products will result in an injury to the consumer's life or property, owes a duty to the consumer to take that reasonable care."

The term "products" includes not only comestibles, but such diverse items as lifts, hair-dye, motor vehicles, chemicals and underpants. The manufacturer's duty extends to the packaging of the product and to any labels, warnings or instructions for use which accompany it (*Vacwell Engineering Co. Ltd v. B. D. H. Chemicals Ltd.* (H.C., 1971)). If the manufacturer of a finished product incorporates a component made by another, he is under a duty to check on its suitability and may be liable for failure to do so should it turn out to be defective (*Winward v. TVR Engineering* (C.A., 1986)). Where products are already in circulation when the defect is discovered the manufacturer must take reasonable steps to warn of the danger or to recall the products (*Walton v. British Leyland (U.K.) Ltd* (H.C., 1978)).

Manufacturer and ultimate consumer

The term "manufacturer" has been judicially interpreted to include any person who actively does something to the goods to create the danger, such as assemblers, servicers, repairers, installers and erectors. In *Malfroot v. Noxal Ltd.* (H.C., 1935) an assembler was held liable when the side-car which he had negligently fitted to a motor-cycle came adrift and injured the plaintiff. Mere suppliers may also come within the rule, even though they may be unaware of the danger and do nothing positive to create it. Thus, in *Andrews v. Hopkinson* (H.C., 1957) a second-hand car dealer was liable for failing to check that an 18-year-old car was roadworthy, with the result that the plaintiff was injured in a collision caused by a failure of the steering. Similarly, in *Fisher v. Harrods* (H.C., 1966) a retailer was held liable for supplying dangerous goods without first checking upon the reputability of his supplier.

Apart from the end user of the product, an "ultimate consumer" is any person who may foreseeably be affected by it. In *Stennett v. Hancock and Peters* (H.C., 1939) the defendant was held liable for negligently fitting a metal flange to the wheel of a lorry, so that it came off while the vehicle was in motion and struck the plaintiff.

Intermediate examination and causation

The normal rules of causation and remoteness apply (see Chap. 4) and, as elsewhere in negligence, difficulties may arise where the negligence of two or more defendants causes indivisible damage. According to Lord Atkin's formulation of the rule, the duty only arises where there is "no reasonable possibility of intermediate examination," which would suggest that there is no duty where such a possibility exists. From a conceptual point of view, however, it is perhaps preferable to deal with the issue of intermediate examination in terms of causation. Thus, failure by an intermediary to make an examination reasonably expected of him may either break the chain of causation (assuming that the examination would, or should, have revealed the defect) or, given that the manufacturer originally created the danger, both manufacturer and intermediary will be liable, as in the Irish case of *Power v. Bedford Motor Co.* (1959). What is clear is that, if the intermediary's failure to examine is to be regarded as severing the causal chain, it must at least have been likely that an examination would be made, so that a mere foreseeable possibility of inspection will not suffice

(*Griffiths v. Arch Engineering Co. Ltd* (H.C., 1968)). If, of course, the intermediary acquires actual knowledge of the defect and fails to withdraw the product from circulation, the manufacturer will probably escape liability (*Taylor v. Rover Co. Ltd.* (H.C., 1966)), just as he will where the intermediary ignores a clear warning to test the product before use (*Kubach v. Hollands* (H.C., 1937)).

Apart from anything that the intermediary may do in relation to the product, regard must equally be had to what the consumer himself does. Failure by the plaintiff to conduct an expected examination or, *a fortiori*, continued use of the product after discovery of the defect, may produce one of two consequences, depending upon the degree of fault. Either the chain of causation will be broken (see, *e.g.* *Farr v. Butters Bros.* (C.A., 1932)), or the loss may be apportioned under the Law Reform (Contributory Negligence) Act 1945. The plaintiff will not be barred from recovery, however, where he has no effective choice in assuming a risk created by a defect of which he is aware (*Denny v. Supplies and Transport Co Ltd.* (C.A., 1950)).

Proof of negligence and damage

The burden rests upon the plaintiff as in any other negligence action; however, despite judicial reluctance to allow the application of *res ipsa loquitor* (see Chap. 3), damage caused by a defect in manufacture, as distinct from a defect in design, may easily give rise to an inference of negligence (*Grant v. Australian Knitting Mills Ltd.* P.C.,1936)). On the other hand, if it is equally probable that the defect arose after the manufacturing process and is wholly unconnected with anything that the manufacturer may have done, the plaintiff will fail (*Evans v. Triplex Safety Glass Co.* (H.C., 1936)). The defendant will no longer escape liability, however, merely by showing that he had a fool-proof system of manufacture and quality control, because the very fact of the defect may be evidence of negligence in the operation of the system by a servant for whom the defendant is vicariously liable (*Hill v. J. Crowe (Cases) Ltd.* (H.C., 1978)). Where the alleged defect is in relation to the design of the product, the plaintiff may face greater difficulty in that the issue of negligence is to be judged in the light of current knowledge which must be proved to have been such as to render the damage foreseeable (*cf.* the "state of the art" defence under section 4(1) (e) of the Consumer Protection Act 1987 where it is for the defendant to prove that such knowledge did not exist).

As far as damage is concerned, liability exists only in respect of personal injury or damage to other property, though consequential financial loss is also recoverable. Pure economic loss is, however, irrecoverable (*Muirhead v. Industrial Tank Specialities Ltd.* (C.A., 1985)), and it is clear from *Murphy v. Brentwood District Council* (H.L., 1990) that both damage to the product itself and "preventive damage" represented by the cost of avoiding apprehended physical damage to persons or property (*e.g.* by repairing or discarding the product) is regarded as pure economic loss (see further Chap. 2). The difficulty remains of determining the circumstances in which a defective product can be said to have caused damage to "other" property. In *Aswan Engineering Establishment Co. v. Lupdine Ltd* (C.A., 1987) the plaintiffs lost a quantity of waterproofing material when the plastic buckets in which it was contained collapsed as a result of exposure to high temperatures. In an action against the manufacturers of the buckets Lloyd L.J. thought that the contents could be regarded as property distinct from their container, thus bringing the case within *Donoghue v. Stevenson* principles (though the claim failed on other grounds). If this analysis is correct the plaintiff would seem to be in a better position at common law than under the 1987 Act (see section 5(2)).

7. EMPLOYER'S LIABILITY AT COMMON LAW

This chapter is concerned with an employer's liability for common law negligence to his employees; the incidence of his vicarious liability for the torts of his employees is dealt with in Chapter 14. Since 1948 this country has had a national insurance system providing benefits to the victims of industrial accidents and to those who contract certain prescribed industrial diseases. Although the statutory scheme is not dependent upon proof of fault, it has not led to any diminution in the number of actions brought by employees against their employers. In addition to his common law duty there is a large body of statutory obligations cast upon the employer for the protection of his workmen, and it is not uncommon for an employee to sue both in negligence and for breach of statutory duty (see Chap. 9). No civil action will lie, however, for breach by an employer of his statutory duty to insure against his liability to his workforce as required by section 1 of the Employers' Liability (Compulsory Insurance) Act 1969 (*Richardson v. Pitt-Stanley* (C.A., 1995)).

THE NATURE OF THE DUTY

At one time, by the doctrine of common employment, there was an implied term in a contract of service that an employee accepted risks incidental to his employment. One of those risks was that he might be injured by the negligence of a fellow employee for whom the employer was not, therefore, vicariously liable. As means were sought to mitigate the harshness of the doctrine, the concept developed of the personal nature of the duty owed by an employer to his workforce – a duty, in other words, which could not be discharged merely by entrusting its performance to another, no matter how apparently competent that other might be. Although the doctrine was abolished in 1948, the employer's personal duty survives and co-exists with his vicarious liability. Traditionally, the duty is said to be threefold, as explained in the leading case of *Wilsons and Clyde Coal Co. Ltd. v. English* (H.L., 1938), namely "the provision of a competent staff of men, adequate material and a proper system and effective supervision." The duty is not absolute but is discharged by the exercise of reasonable care and is thus similar to the duty of care in the tort of negligence generally. Although most of the cases concern work accidents, the duty clearly extends to guarding against disease and gradual deterioration in health as a result of adverse working conditions (*Thompson v. Smith's Shiprepairers (North Shields) Ltd* (H.C., 1984)); but it does not extend to the prevention of economic loss by, for example, advising the employee to take out insurance (*Reid v. Rush & Tomkins Group plc* (C.A., 1989)), nor to the prevention of injury to health caused by self-induced intoxication (*Barrett v. Ministry of Defence* (C.A., 1995)). The various aspects of the duty will now be considered.

Competent staff

The abolition of the doctrine of common employment has drastically reduced the significance of this particular aspect of the duty, since an employee will usually be able to sue his employer vicariously for the wrongdoings of a colleague. It remains important, however, where the wrongful act, such as an assault or violent horseplay, takes place outside the course of employment. In this case the employer may be liable for breach of his personal duty if he knew or ought to have known of his employee's vicious or playful tendencies (*Hudson v. Ridge Manufacturing Co. Ltd.* (H.C., 1957)). So, too, if an employee is instructed to perform a task for which he has not been properly trained and thereby injures his workmate, the employer may be liable, even though there might be difficulty in establishing negligence by the employee for the purposes of vicarious liability.

Safe plant and equipment

The duty here is to take reasonable care to provide proper plant and equipment and to maintain them as such. This includes the provision of protective devices and clothing, and, in appropriate cases, a warning or exhortation from the employer to make use of such equipment (*Pape v. Cumbria County Council* (H.C., 1992)). In *Bux v. Slough Metals Ltd.* (C.A., 1973) the plaintiff foundry worker lost the sight of one eye when splashed with molten metal. Although the employer had, in compliance with statutory regulations binding upon him, provided protective goggles, he was held liable for breach of his common law duty, which extended to persuading and even insisting upon the use of protective equipment. This case also demonstrates that compliance with a statutory obligation, whilst evidence of a discharge of the common law duty, is not conclusive of the matter. Most employees will now be protected by the Personal Protective Equipment at Work Regulations 1992, which impose a statutory duty to take all reasonable steps to see that protective equipment is properly used, though it is the employee's duty to use it.

With regard to injury caused by defective equipment, it was held in *Davie v. New Merton Board Mills Ltd.* (H.L., 1959) that the duty to provide proper tools was satisfied by purchase from a reputable supplier. The decision has now been reversed, however, by the Employers' Liability (Defective Equipment) Act 1969, which renders an employer personally liable in negligence if two conditions are met: first, that the employee is injured in the course of his employment by a defect in equipment issued by the employer for the purposes of the employer's business and, secondly, that the defect is attributable wholly or partly to the fault of a third party (whether identifiable or not). Strict liability is thus imposed upon the employer if his employee can prove that some third party, such as the manufacturer, was at fault, though contributory negligence is a defence. The manufacturer may now, of course, be strictly liable under the Consumer Protection Act 1987 (see Chap. 6), but this does not in any way affect the employer's position under the 1969 Act. In *Coltman v. Bibby Tankers Ltd.* (H.L., 1988) "equipment" for the purposes of the Act was widely defined to include a ship. It was further held in *Knowles v. Liverpool City Council* (H.L., 1993) that the word embraced any material furnished by the employer for the purposes of his business and was not confined to such things as tools and machinery, and their Lordships also considered that the Act would apply even though the employee was neither required to use, nor had in fact used, the equipment in question.

Apart from the 1969 Act the employee may be able to rely on the Provision and Use of Work Equipment Regulations 1992 which provide, inter alia, that employers must ensure that work equipment is so constructed or adapted as to be suitable for the purpose for which it is used or provided, and that such equipment is maintained in an efficient state, in efficient working order and in good repair. The definition of "work equipment", however, is not as wide as under the 1969 Act.

Safe system of work

This is the expression used to describe such matters as the organisation of the work, the manner in which it is to be carried out, the number of men required for a particular task and the part that each is to play, the taking ,of safety precautions, and the giving of special instructions, particularly to inexperienced workers (see *Speed v. Thomas Swift & Co. Ltd.* (C.A., 1943)). In *Johnstone v. Bloomsbury Health Authority* (C.A., 1991) it was held that requiring the plaintiff to work such long hours as might foreseeably injure his health could constitute a breach of duty, although a majority expressed the view that the implied contractual duty to take reasonable care for an employee's safety is subject to any express term imposing an absolute duty to work certain specified hours. In *Walker v. Northumberland County Council* (H.C., 1995) the plaintiff suffered a nervous breakdown as a result of work pressure. Before returning to work it was agreed that assistance would be provided to reduce his workload. In the event very little was provided, and he suffered a second breakdown which forced him to stop work permanently. His employers were held liable for failing to provide a safe system of work in that they continued to employ him without adequate additional assistance. Although the duty most commonly arises where the work is of a routine or repetitive nature, it also applies where only an isolated act of a particular kind is to be performed, especially if the operation is of a complicated or unusual character (*Winter v. Cardiff R.D.C* (H.L., 1950)). The employer does not discharge his duty merely by providing a safe system unless he also takes reasonable steps to see that it is put into operation, and he must be mindful of the fact that workers are often careless of their own safety. On the other hand, it may not be necessary to warn or advise an experienced worker of the risks with which he should be familiar. Even though the employer has devised a safe system, he will be liable upon proof of a negligent failure to put it into practice (*McDermid v. Nash Dredging and Reclamation Co Ltd.* (H.L., 1987)).

Safe premises

It is clear that the employer's obligation includes making the premises as safe as the exercise of reasonable care and skill permits, but he is not required to eliminate every foreseeable risk if the burden in so doing is too onerous (*Latimer v. A.E.C. Ltd.* (H.L., 1953)). In *Wilson v. Tyneside Window Cleaning Co.* (C.A., 1958) it was held that the duty exists equally in relation to premises in the occupation or control of a third party. In appropriate circumstances an employer may therefore be expected to go and inspect the premises to see that they are reasonably safe for the work to be done upon them; but the fact that the employer does not have control of the premises is important in determining whether he has been negligent. As far as this aspect of the duty is concerned, most work-places are now likely to be governed by the Workplace (Health, Safety and Welfare) Regulations 1992.

THE SCOPE OF THE DUTY

The duty arises only where the master-servant relationship exists so that it will not, for example, avail an independent contractor. It extends to those acts which are reasonably incidental to the employment and is owed to each employee individually, the consequence of which is that the personal circumstances of the employee must be taken into account, in so far as the employer knew or ought to have known of them. Thus, in *Paris v. Stepney B. C.* (H.L., 1951) it was held that, where a garage worker known by his employer to be one-eyed was engaged on work involving a risk of injury to his remaining eye, the employer was under a duty to provide him with goggles. Finally, although the duty is frequently dealt with under its various sub-headings, it is to be remembered that there is in effect but a single duty to take reasonable care in the conduct of operations so as not to subject employees to unnecessary risks.

DELEGATION

Since the duty is personal it is said to be non-delegable, so that the employer does not discharge his obligation by entrusting its performance to another, whether that other be a servant or independent contractor (*Wilsons and Clyde Coal Co. Ltd. v. English* (H.L., 1938)). Although, as far as the employment of contractors is concerned, some doubt was cast upon this proposition by *Davie v. New Merton Board Mills Ltd.* (H.L., 1959), the widely accepted view is that an employer who entrusts performance of his duty to a person other than a servant remains responsible for the defaults of that person (*McDermid v. Nash Dredging & Reclamation Co. Ltd.* (H.L., 1987); see, too, Employers' Liability (Defective Equipment) Act 1969).

8. OCCUPIER'S LIABILITY

THE OCCUPIERS' LIABILITY ACT 1957

The liability of an occupier in respect of loss or injury suffered by those who come lawfully upon his premises is primarily governed by the 1957 Act. Although it is clear that the duty imposed by the Act arises where damage results from the static condition of the premises, there is some doubt as to whether it applies where the plaintiff is injured in consequence of an activity conducted upon the premises. The balance of authority would suggest that it does, at least where the activity in question is an integral purpose of the occupation, rather than being merely ancillary to it. In any event, since the statutory duty is to take reasonable care, there is little or no difference between an action under the Act and one for breach of the common law duty care.

Section 2(1) of the Act provides: "An occupier owes the same duty, the 'common duty of care,' to all his visitors, except in so far as he is free to and does extend, restrict, modify or exclude his duty to any visitor or visitors by agreement or otherwise."

The occupier
The Act contains no definition of "occupier" which is simply a term of convenience to denote a person who has a sufficient degree of control over premises to put him under a duty of care towards those who come lawfully on to the premises (*Wheat v. Lacon & Co. Ltd* (H.L., 1966)). Control is thus the decisive factor, and it is immaterial that the occupier has no interest in the land. He may be an

owner in occupation, a tenant, a licensee or any person having the right to possession and to permit others to enter the premises. For example, in *AMF International Ltd v. Magnet Bowling Ltd* (H.C., 1968) building contractors were held to be joint occupiers along with the building owners. But a landlord who lets premises by demise to a tenant is not the occupier thereof for the purposes of the Act, though he remains the occupier of those parts of the premises excluded from the demise, such as an entrance hall or common staircase in a block of flats (*Moloney v. Lambeth London B.C.* (H.C., 1966)). Exclusive occupation is not, however, essential, so that there may be more than one occupier of the same premises or part of the premises. The issue of multiple occupation was fully considered in the leading case of *Wheat v. Lacon & Co. Ltd* where the House of Lords held that the residential area of licensed premises was occupied both by the manager who lived there under licence from the brewers, and by the brewers, who could be regarded as occupying either vicariously through their servant (the manager) or because they retained control. It was also made clear that, although two or more people may owe the same common duty of care, the content of their duty might well differ according to the degree of control exercised.

The premises
By section 1(3)(a) of the Act, the statutory provisions extend to any fixed or movable structure, including any vessel, vehicle or aircraft. This is apt to include not only structures of a permanent nature but temporary erections such as ladders and scaffolding. But with regard to "vessels, vehicles and aircraft" the Act would appear to apply only to the structural state of the premises, so that where injury is caused to a passenger by, say, negligent driving, the appropriate cause of action is negligence at common law.

Visitors
The statutory duty is owed only to visitors who, by section 1(2), are those who would, at common law, have been either invitees or licensees. The common law distinction between these two categories of entrant is thereby abolished and the vital distinction (which remains unaffected by the Act) is as between the visitor and the trespasser. No difficulty arises where the occupier expressly invites or permits another to enter or use his premises, bearing in mind that such invitation or permission may legitimately be limited either to a particular part of the premises or for a specified purpose. It may be alleged, however, that the occupier has impliedly

sanctioned the entry, and whether this is so is a question to be decided on the facts of each case. A tradesman, for example, has an implied licence to walk along a garden path to the front door for the purpose of promoting his business with the occupier, unless of course he has been clearly forbidden to do so. For a licence to be inferred there must be evidence that the occupier has permitted entry as opposed to merely tolerated it, for there is no positive obligation to keep the trespasser out. Moreover, repeated trespass of itself confers no licence (*Edwards v. Railway Executive* (H.L., 1952)). It must be said that in some cases the courts have been at pains to infer the existence of a licence. Thus, in *Lowery v. Walker* (H.L., 1911), members of the public had for many years used the defendant's field as a short cut to the railway station. The defendant had not infrequently prevented them from so doing, but did nothing further until, without warning, he turned a savage horse in the field. The animal attacked and injured the plaintiff, who succeeded in his action on the basis that he was a licensee, not a trespasser. This, and other cases, were decided at a time when trespassers were afforded little or no protection and, in view of the more favourable treatment which they now receive (see later in this chapter), the courts may be less favourably inclined to find an implied licence in a case such as *Lowery*.

Three further types of entrant must now be considered. First, those who enter premises for any purpose in the exercise of a right conferred by law are, by section 2(6) of the Act, treated as having the occupier's permission to be there for that purpose (whether they in fact have it or not) and are therefore owed the common duty of care. Secondly, section 5(1) provides that where a person enters under the terms of a contract with the occupier there is, in the absence of express provision in the contract, an implied term that the entrant is owed the common duty of care and, according to *Sole v. W. J. Hallt Ltd.* (H.C., 1973)), he may frame his claim either in contract or under the 1957 Act. It is further provided by section 3(1) that where a person contracts with the occupier on the basis that a third party is to have access to the premises, the duty owed by the occupier to such third party as his visitor cannot be reduced by the terms of the contract to a level lower than the common duty of care. Conversely, if the contract imposes upon the occupier any obligation which exceeds the requirements of the statutory duty, then the third party is entitled to the benefit of that additional obligation. Thirdly, those who use public (*Greenhalgh v. British Railways Board* (C.A., 1969)) or private (*Holden v. White* (C.A., 1982)) rights of way are not visitors for the purposes of the 1957

Act, though the user of a private right of way is now owed a duty under the Occupiers' Liability Act 1984 (see later in this chapter). An owner of land over which a public right of way passes may be liable for misfeasance, but not negligent nonfeasance (*McGeown v. Northern Ireland Housing Executive* (H.L., 1994)).

Exclusion of the duty

It has already been seen that the duty owed to a contractual entrant is governed by the terms of the contract and that a person who enters under a contract to which he is not a party is owed, as a minimum, the common duty of care. In the case of non-contractual entrants it is clear that, at common law, an occupier may be able to exclude or limit his liability by notice, provided that reasonable steps are taken to bring it to the visitor's attention and that, upon its proper construction, it is clear and unambiguous. Such was the decision in *Ashdown v. Samuel Williams & Sons* (C.A., 1956), where it was held that the plaintiff, who was injured by the negligent shunting of a railway wagon upon the defendant's premises, was defeated in her claim by exclusion notices erected by the defendant stating that persons entered at their own risk and that no liability would be accepted for injury or damage, whether caused by negligence or otherwise.

Despite the criticisms of *Ashdown*'s case, section 2(1) of the 1957 Act clearly envisages the possibility of an exclusion of the duty and the decision was followed by a majority in *White v. Blackmore* (C.A., 1972). The principle is said to rest upon the basis that if an occupier can prevent people from entering his premises, then he can equally impose conditions, subject to which entry is permitted. It will almost certainly not therefore apply either where the visitor enters in the exercise of a right conferred by law, or where he has, in practical terms, no real freedom of choice (as, for example, where an employee enters the premises in the ordinary course of his employment: *Burnett v. British Waterways Board* (C.A., 1973)). Furthermore, some writers have argued that the *Ashdown* principle no longer applies in its full rigour on the ground that, if the duty owed to a trespasser (see later in this chapter) represents a minimum standard below which the occupier cannot go, then that duty must also be owed to all entrants; for to suggest otherwise would be to accord to the trespasser a protection denied to the lawful visitor.

Whatever the present common law position may be, the power of the occupier to exclude or restrict his liability for negligence has been severely reduced by the Unfair Contract Terms Act 1977.

Section 2 of the Act provides that a person cannot, by reference to a contract term or to a notice, exclude or restrict his liability for death or personal injury caused by negligence; and, in the case of other loss or damage, he cannot exclude or restrict his liability for negligence unless the term or notice satisfies the requirement of reasonableness. By section 1(1) negligence includes a breach of the common duty of care imposed by the 1957 Act and it matters not whether liability arises directly or vicariously. More importantly, the operation of section 2 of the 1977 Act is confined to those situations where there is "business liability" which is defined in section 1(3) as liability for breach of duty arising from things done in the course of a business or from the occupation of premises used for the business purposes of the occupier. There is no exhaustive definition of "business" though section 14 provides that it includes a profession and the activities of any government department or local or public authority. It should also be noted that section 1(3) has been modified by section 2 of the Occupiers' Liability Act 1984 which enables a business occupier to exclude liability to those whom he allows on to his land for recreational or educational purposes, provided that it is not part of this business to grant access for such purposes.

As a result of these provisions *Ashdown*'s case would be decided differently today. But whether *White v. Blackmore* (C.A., 1972) is similarly affected is debatable, because in that case private land was used to stage a fund-raising event for charity, and it is not certain whether that would be classed as a business occupation.

The common duty of care

The common duty of care is defined in section 2(2) as "a duty to take such care as in all circumstances of the case is reasonable to see that the visitor will be reasonably safe in using the premises for the purposes for which he is invited or permitted to be there." This is similar to the common law duty of care, and may extend to taking steps to see that a visitor does not deliberately harm other visitors by foreseeably likely misconduct (*Cunninghams v. Reading Football Club Ltd* (H.C., 1991)). Whether the occupier has discharged it depends upon the facts, taking into account such matters as the nature of the danger, the purpose of the visit and the knowledge of the parties. In particular, there is express provision in the Act relating to children, those with special skills, warning notices and independent contractors, and these will now be considered in turn.

1. Children

The Act provides that the amount of care, or of lack of it, which the occupier may expect in the visitor is a relevant consideration, so that, by section 2(3)(a), the occupier must be prepared for children to be less careful than adults. At common law, where a child was injured by some especially attractive but potentially dangerous object which had allured him on to the land, the occupier could not be heard to say that the child was a trespasser in relation to the very thing which had attracted him in the first place. In *Glasgow Corp. v. Taylor* (H.L., 1922), for example, a child of seven died after eating some poisonous berries which he had picked from a bush in a public park. The berries had a very tempting appearance to children, yet the defendant, though aware of their toxic nature, had neither erected a barrier around the bush nor given any warning. It was held that there was a good cause of action. If, on the other hand, there is no dangerous object or allurement upon the land the occupier will not normally be liable (*Latham v. R. Johnson & Nephew Ltd* (C.A., 1913)). Nor is he liable if adequate warning is given to keep away, or the danger is one which should be obvious even to a child.

In the case of very young children, to whom many ordinarily harmless things may pose a potential hazard, the courts at one time applied the doctrine of the conditional licence, a legal fiction whereby the child was regarded as a trespasser unless accompanied by a responsible guardian. A different approach was adopted, however, in *Phipps v. Rochester Corp.* (H.C., 1955) in which the court considered that it was proper to have regard to the habits of prudent parents who will, where appropriate, either take steps to satisfy themselves that the place holds no danger for children, or not permit the child to wander without supervision. This case was followed in *Simkiss v. Rhondda B.C.* (C.A., 1983) and is clearly consonant with the provisions of the 1957 Act which state that, in determining whether the occupier has discharged his duty, regard is to be had to all the circumstances. One of those circumstances must be what the occupier is reasonably entitled to expect of a young child's parents.

2. Special skills

Section 2(3)(b) provides that "an occupier may expect that a person, in the exercise of his calling, will appreciate and guard against any special risks ordinarily incident to it, so far as the occupier leaves him free to do so." Thus, in *Roles v. Nathan* (C.A., 1963) the defendant was held not liable for the death of two chimney sweeps killed by carbon monoxide fumes while sealing up a flue in the defendant's boiler. Had they suffered injury by falling through a rotten floorboard the position would, of course, have been otherwise (*Woolins v. British Celanese Ltd* (C.A., 1966)). In *Salmon v. Seafarer Restaurants Ltd* (H.C., 1983) a fireman was entitled to recover damages when it was reasonably foreseeable that he would be injured while fighting a blaze caused by the occupier's negligence, despite the exercise of his special skills (approved in *Ogwo v. Taylor* (H.L., 1988)).

3. Warnings

The occupier may, in accordance with section 2(4)(a) of the Act, discharge his duty by warning his visitor of the particular danger, provided that the warning is sufficient to enable the visitor to be reasonably safe. Warning notices should be distinguished from exclusion notices. By sufficient warning the occupier discharges his duty, whereas an exclusion purports to take away the right of recovery in respect of a breach. To be effective a warning must sufficiently identify the source of the danger and be brought adequately to the visitor's notice. Mere knowledge of the nature and extent of the risk is not necessarily a bar to recovery, though it may go towards establishing a defence of *volenti non fit injuria* or, more likely, contributory negligence (*Bunker v. Charles Brand & Son Ltd* (H.C., 1969); see Chap. 5).

4. Independent contractors

Where a visitor suffers damage due to faulty construction, maintenance or repair work by an independent contractor employed by the occupier, section 2(4)(b) provides that the occupier will not be liable if it was reasonable to entrust the work to a contractor and he took such steps (if any) as he reasonably ought to see that the contractor was competent and had done the work properly. Assuming, therefore, that the occupier reasonably entrusted the work to a contractor whom he had checked to see was suitably qualified to do the job, he will not be liable for that contractor's defaults provided that he took reasonable steps, where necessary, to satisfy himself that the work was properly done. The occupier is not necessarily expected to check work of a technical nature (*e.g.* lift maintenance as in *Haseldine v. Daw & Son Ltd* (C.A., 1941)), but in the case of a complex project he may be under a duty to have the contractor's work supervised by a qualified specialist such as an architect or surveyor (*AMF International Ltd v. Magnet Bowling Ltd*

(H.C., 1968)). Where the work is of a routine nature requiring no particular skill or expertise, the occupier may himself be expected to check it and will be liable for failing to do so (*Woodward v. Mayor of Hastings* (C.A., 1945)). On a point of interpretation it was held in *Ferguson v. Welsh* (H.L., 1987) that the word "construction" in section 2(4)(b) was wide enough to embrace demolition and that the provision protected an occupier from liability for injuries to visitors not only after completion of the work, but also during its execution. The majority also held that where an occupier had notice of an unsafe system of work adopted by the contractor, he could be liable to an employee of the contractor injured thereby, although two of their Lordships thought that any such liability would be *qua* joint tortfeasor rather than occupier.

Damage

By section 1(3)(b) of the Act, the statutory provisions apply not only to personal injury but also to damage to property, including the property of those who are not visitors which is nevertheless lawfully on the premises. In *AMF International Ltd v. Magnet Bowling Ltd* (H.C., 1968) it was held that financial loss consequential upon damage to property is also recoverable.

Defences

The provisions of the Law Reform (Contributory Negligence) Act 1945 apply and section 2(5) of the 1957 Act provides that an occupier is not liable in respect of risks which the visitor willingly accepts, thus allowing for the defence of *volenti non fit injuria* (see Chap. 5). However, where there is business liability within the meaning of the Unfair Contract Terms Act 1977, section 2(3) of that Act provides that a person's agreement to or awareness of a notice purporting to exclude liability for negligence is not of itself to be taken as indicating his voluntary acceptance of any risk.

THE OCCUPIERS' LIABILITY ACT 1984

Persons to whom the Act applies

The 1984 Act governs the liability of an occupier to "persons other than his visitors" in respect of injury suffered by them on the premises due to the state of the premises or to things done or omitted to be done upon them. The terms "occupier" and "premises" have the same meanings as for the purposes of the Occupiers' Liability Act 1957. The expression "persons other than his visitors" includes trespassers and persons exercising private rights of way, but those using public rights of way are specifically excluded.

The scope of the duty

Section 1(3) of the 1984 Act provides that the occupier owes a duty if:

    (a) he is aware of the danger or has reasonable grounds to believe that it exists;

    (b) he knows or has reasonable grounds to believe that the non-visitor is in the vicinity of the danger concerned or that he may come into the vicinity of the danger; and

    (c) the risk is one against which, in all the circumstances of the case, he may reasonably be expected to offer the non-visitor some protection.

Whilst paragraph (c) clearly adopts an objective test, it would appear that paragraphs (a) and (b) import a subjective element in that the existence of the duty depends upon the occupier's actual knowledge of facts which should lead him to conclude that a danger exists or that the non-visitor is in the vicinity. If the occupier is not aware of those facts he may not owe a duty, even though a reasonable occupier would have known of them. Such an interpretation is not far removed from the old common law duty of "common humanity" which took into account, along with the occupier's skill and resources, his actual knowledge of the trespasser's presence or of the likelihood of it (*British Railways Board v. Herrington* (H.L., 1972)). Although it seems, from the objective wording of paragraph (c), that the individual occupier's skill and resources no longer come into the equation, the position is not entirely clear as regards what knowledge is required. For the purposes of section 1(3)(*b*) the fact that the occupier has erected a fence to keep people out does not mean that he had reasonable grounds to believe that they would enter the premises (*White v. St. Albans City Council* (C.A., 1990)).

Where the duty arises section 1(4) states that the duty is to take such care as is reasonable in all the circumstances of the case to see that the non-visitor does not suffer injury on the premises by reason of the danger concerned. This is the usual standard in negligence generally, and whether the occupier has discharged his duty will depend upon the character of the entry, the age of the non-visitor, and the extent of the risk, including the burden that would be imposed upon the occupier in eliminating it.

It is to be noted that the new statutory duty applies only to personal injury or death. Liability for loss of, or damage to, property is expressly excluded by section 1(8).

Defences

Section 1(5) of the Act provides that the occupier may, in appropriate cases, discharge his duty by taking reasonable steps to warn of the danger or to discourage persons from incurring the risk. Whether a warning is effective will depend among other things upon the nature of the risk and the age of the entrant. What is adequate for an adult may not be so for a child, particularly if the danger is an allurement.

The defence of *volenti non fit injuria* is preserved by section 1(6) of the Act. It remains to be seen whether it will be more readily available as against trespassers, though there seems no reason why it should be. In any event the indication in *Titchener v. British Railways Board* (H.L., 1983) is that it will normally be limited to dangers arising from the state of the premises.

Although the Act is silent on the matter, there is nothing to suggest that contributory negligence may not be a defence.

Exclusion notices

There is no mention in the Act of the possibility of excluding liability to the non-visitor, and the provisions of the Unfair Contract Terms Act 1977 do not apply to the 1984 duty. Trespassers pose particular problems because, depending upon the point at which they enter the premises, they may be less likely to see a notice than a lawful visitor. One suggested solution is that the duty under the 1984 Act is a minimum which cannot be excluded so that even the lawful visitor would be protected by it, even though he was aware of an exclusion notice (put up, for example, by a non-business occupier). The objection to this, it has been said, is that it would effectively deprive the occupier of his right to exclude liability entirely as against the lawful visitor, which right was given in the 1957 Act and was left intact, at least for the non-business occupier, by the 1977 Unfair Contract Terms Act.

Liability of non-occupier to trespasser

At common law, the liability of a non-occupier (such as a contractor) to the trespasser rests upon ordinary negligence principles. The fact that the plaintiff is a trespasser in relation to the occupier is not relevant except in so far as the trespasser's presence may be less foreseeable. Thus in *Buckland v. Guildford Gas Light and*

Coke Co. (H.C., 1949) the defendants, who had erected electricity cables on a farmer's land close to the top of a tree, were held liable for the death of a young girl who climbed the tree and was electrocuted. This decision is unaffected by the 1984 Act, but there are indications in *Herrington*'s case that no distinction should be drawn in this respect between occupiers and non-occupiers, in which case the defendants in *Buckland* would now owe the duty of common humanity.

9. BREACH OF STATUTORY DUTY

Breach by the defendant of an obligation cast upon him by statute (other than one which expressly seeks to impose liability in tort) may, apart from giving rise to any criminal sanction laid down in the Act, also enable a person injured by the breach to bring a civil action for damages for "breach of statutory duty." This is a tort in its own right independent of any other form of tortious liability. Whether a plaintiff can sue depends on whether the statute, upon its proper construction, confers a right of civil action upon him and this is, in theory at least, a question of ascertaining the intention of Parliament.

WAS A RIGHT OF ACTION INTENDED?

As a preliminary step, then, the plaintiff must prove that the legislature intended to create a right to sue. In a few instances Parliament has expressly made known its intention, but in the majority of cases the statute is silent on the issue. It is then for the courts to interpret the enactment in order to discover what that intention is and, to this end, certain guidelines have been established. It should be said at the outset, however, that there is considerable inconsistency in judicial approach to the problem, because, as Lord Browne-Wilkinson observed in *X. v. Bedfordshire County Council* (H.L., 1995), although the general principles applicable in determining whether an action lies are well established, the application of those principles in any particular case remains difficult. The following paragraph contains his Lordship's summary of the principles.

The basic proposition is that a breach of statutory duty does not, by itself, give rise to a private law action. Such an action will arise, however, if it can be shown that, on the proper construction of the statute, the duty was imposed for the protection of a limited class of the public and that Parliament intended to confer upon members of that class a right to sue for breach. There is no general rule for determining whether the Act does create such a right, but if no other remedy is provided for its breach that is an indicator in the plaintiff's favour. If the Act does contain other provision for enforcing the duty that is an indication of an intention that it was to be enforced by those means alone and not by private law action (*Cutler v. Wandsworth Stadium Ltd* (H.L., 1949); *Lonrho Ltd v. Shell Petroleum Co. Ltd (No. 2)* (H.L. 1982)). However, the mere existence of some other statutory remedy is not decisive, since it is still possible to show that the protected class was intended to have a private remedy. A classic example is that a civil action will lie for breach of industrial safety regulations imposed upon employers, despite the imposition of criminal penalties (*Groves v. Lord Wimborne* (C.A., 1898)). In *X. v. Bedfordshire County Council* two sets of appeals came before the House of Lords relating in the one set to an alleged breach of a local authority's statutory duties in respect of child welfare, and in the other of its duties with regard to the provision of education for children with special needs. It was held that, as in the case of legislation regulating the conduct of prisons (see *Hague v. Deputy Governor of Parkhurst Prison* (H.L., 1991)), no civil action lay on the grounds, *inter alia*, that although the legislation did in fact protect individuals adversely affected by the local authorities' activities, it was intended not for the benefit of those individuals but of society as a whole. Lord Browne-Wilkinson said that cases where a right of action has been held to arise are all cases in which the duty has been very limited and specific as opposed to general administrative functions imposed on public bodies, involving the exercise of administrative discretion.

In conclusion, in determining whether, in any particular case, a civil action for breach of statutory duty will lie, the starting point is to look to precedent or for a clearly stated Parliamentary intention. In the absence of either, the above principles may assist, but it is in all cases a question of ascertaining the fundamental purpose the legislation intended to achieve, and that can only be done by a consideration of the enactment as a whole.

THE ELEMENTS OF THE TORT

Duty owed to the plaintiff

In establishing that breach of the particular duty will in principle
ground a right of action the plaintiff will in most, if not all, cases
have established that the obligation was imposed for the benefit of
a limited class. He must then prove that, on the proper construction of the statutory provision, he is a member of that class. In
Hartley v. Mayoh & Co. (C.A., 1954) the widow of a fireman electrocuted while fighting a fire at the defendants' factory had no cause
of action because the regulations existed for the benefit of "persons
employed", and her husband was not such a person. Similarly the
expression "person employed or working on the premises" was held
in *Napieralski v. Curtis (Contractors) Ltd* (H.C., 1959) not to include a
person working for his own private purposes and after normal
working hours. In contrast, the same expression has been held to
cover a worker who was not acting within the course of his employment but was on a frolic of his own (*Uddin v. Associated Portland
Cement Manufacturers Ltd* (C.A., 1965), approved in *Westwood v. Post
Office* (H.L., 1974), where the plaintiff was a trespasser on that part
of the premises to which the action related).

Defendant in breach of duty

The plaintiff must prove that the defendant was in breach, and this
can only be ascertained by having regard to the precise wording of
the Act to determine the nature of the obligation. Some obligations
are absolute, such as that contained in section 14(1) of the Factories Act 1961 requiring that "every dangerous part of any machinery
shall be securely fenced", so that whether reasonable care was
taken is irrelevant (see *John Summers & Sons Ltd v. Frost* (H.L. 1955),
where compliance with the regulation would have rendered the
machine unusable). Other safety provisions require measures to be
taken "so far as is reasonably practicable", which is similar to the
ordinary common law negligence formula with the important proviso that the burden is upon the defendant to prove that compliance was not reasonably practicable (*Nimmo v. Alexander Cowan &
Sons Ltd* (H.L., 1967); *Larner v. British Steel plc* (C.A., 1993)).

It is to be noted that the provisions of the Factories Act and of
other work safety legislation have been, or are in the process of
being, replaced by a unified series of regulations pertaining to particular aspects of work. As with the old legislation some of the
duties contained in the regulations impose an absolute obligation,

while others are qualified in some way, so similar problems of interpretation are likely to arise.

Damage of the contemplated type

For the plaintiff to succeed the harm suffered must be of a type
which the Act was designed to prevent. In *Gorris v. Scott* (Ex., 1874)
the plaintiff's sheep were swept overboard the defendant's vessel
during a storm. The sheep were not penned contrary to statutory
regulations, but the plaintiff nevertheless failed in his action
because the object of the regulations was to prevent the spread of
disease, not to afford protection from the perils of the sea. So, too,
it has been held that the aim of the fencing provisions of the Factories Acts is to prevent the operator from coming into contact with
the machine and not to stop parts of the machine, or the materials
on which it is working, from flying out and striking the operator
(*Close v. Steel Co. of Wales* (H.L., 1962); *Nicholls v. F. Austin (Leyton)
Ltd* (H.L., 1946)). There has been a tendency in more recent times,
however, to adopt a more flexible approach. In *Donaghey v. Boulton &
Paul Ltd* (H.L., 1968) the plaintiff slipped and fell through an open
space in an asbestos roof on which he was working. In breach of
their duty the defendants had failed to provide him with adequate
crawling boards, but argued that the expressed object of the regulations was to prevent workers from falling through fragile roofing
materials, not through holes in the roof. The House of Lords
rejected such a narrow interpretation and held the defendants
liable. Lord Reid said that if the damage is of a kind which the
regulation seeks to prevent, it matters not that it happens in a
manner not contemplated by the enactment, though this is not easy
to reconcile with the decisions on fencing provisions cited
above.

Causation

The burden rests upon the plaintiff to prove on a balance of probabilities that the breach of statutory duty caused or materially contributed to the damage (*Bonnington Castings Ltd v. Wardlaw* (H.L.,
1956)). In this respect there is no distinction between this tort and
a common law negligence action, so that the plaintiff must show
that he would not have sustained injury but for the defendant's
breach. That this may present difficulties where, as is often the
case with industrial safety legislation, the breach consists of an
omission is illustrated in *McWilliams v. Sir William Arrol & Co. Ltd.*
(H.L., 1962). An experienced workman fell to his death because he
was not wearing a safety harness. Although the employer was in

breach of duty for failing to provide a belt he was held not liable
since, on the evidence, the deceased would probably not have worn
the belt anyway and the accident would still have occurred. At one
time it might have been thought that *McGhee v. National Coal Board*
(H.L., 1973) supported the view that the plaintiff need only establish that the breach materially increased the risk of damage, but it
has now been held that that case decided no more than that the
plaintiff was entitled to succeed upon proof that the breach materially contributed to the damage (see Chap. 4).

The plaintiff must also show that the damage is not too
remote and the usual test of reasonable foresight applies. As in
an action for negligence at common law, the precise way in
which the damage is caused need not be foreseeable, provided
that the other elements of the tort are satisfied (*Millard v. Serck
Tubes Ltd* (C.A., 1969)).

On the issue of causation generally, a particular problem arises
where it is the plaintiff's own wrongful act which puts the
defendant in breach. In *Ginty v. Belmont Building Supplies Ltd*
(H.C., 1959) a regulation binding upon both parties required the
use of crawling boards on fragile roofs. The defendant had provided the boards and given full instructions as to their use to
the plaintiff who, although an experienced workman, neglected
to use them and fell through a roof. Both parties were clearly
in breach of their statutory obligation but it was held that the
plaintiff was the sole author of his injury and his action failed.
The *Ginty* principle is in the nature of a defence which was
explained by Lord Reid in *Boyle v. Kodak Ltd.* (H.L., 1969) in the
following terms: "... once the plaintiff has established that there
was a breach of an enactment which made the employer abso-
lutely liable, and that that breach caused the accident, he need
do no more. But it is then open to the employer to set up a
defence that in fact he was not in any way in fault but that the
plaintiff employee was alone to blame." Even if the plaintiff is
not in breach of his statutory duty he will, for similar reasons,
fail in his action if it is his own deliberate act of folly which
puts the defendant in breach (*Horne v. Lec Refrigeration Ltd* (H.C.,
1965)). The operation of this principle is, however, confined
within narrow limits and it will not avail a defendant who is in
some way personally at fault. The employer who, for example,
fails to provide adequate instructions or supervision or who
acquiesces in the breach will still be liable, though there may
be a reduction for contributory negligence (see *Boyle v. Kodak Ltd*
(above)).

DEFENCES

Volenti non fit injuria

As a matter of public policy this defence is not available to an employer who is sued for a breach of his own statutory duty. In *Imperial Chemical Industries Ltd v. Shatwell* (H.L., 1965) it was held that the defence is available where the plaintiff sues his employer vicariously for the default of a fellow worker, provided that the plaintiff is not of lower rank to, or in the habit of taking orders from, his colleague. In cases other than employer and employee there seems no reason why, in principle, the defence should not be available (see Chap. 5).

Contributory negligence

This is clearly available (see Chap. 5) but, as far as workmen are concerned, the House of Lords in *Caswell v. Powell Duffryn Associated Collieries Ltd* (H.L., 1940) said that regard must be had to the conditions in which they work, bearing in mind the noise, fatigue and repetitive nature of the job. All the same, whilst momentary lapses of concentration may not be too harshly penalised, a finding of contributory negligence is by no means uncommon in this type of case. It is to be noted that whilst a breach by the plaintiff of a statutory duty imposed upon him may well amount to contributory negligence, he is not defeated by the *ex turpi* principle (*National Coal Board v. England* (H.L., 1954); and see Chap. 5).

Delegation

The general rule is that where a duty is imposed upon the defendant, he does not discharge it by entrusting its performance to another. Where, however, the alleged delegation is to the plaintiff himself, that is a relevant factor in deciding the issue of causation. In other words it is not so much a question of whether there has been a delegation, but rather whose fault it was that the damage occurred (Pearson J. in *Ginty*'s case).

---

10. DEFAMATION

Defamation may be defined as the publication of a statement which tends to lower a person in the estimation of right-thinking people generally or which tends to make them shun or avoid him. The latter part of the definition makes it clear that the words need not bring the plaintiff into ridicule or contempt, but may arouse only feelings of pity (*Youssoupoff v. M.G.M. Pictures Ltd* (C.A., 1934)). Although a trading corporation can sue for a defamatory attack upon its commercial reputation (*South Hetton Coal Co. Ltd v. North Eastern News Association Ltd* (C.A., 1894)), local government and other organs of government may not, because to permit otherwise would be to inhibit freedom of speech (*Derbyshire County Council v. Times Newspapers Ltd* (H.L., 1993)). The aim of the law is to strike a balance between freedom of speech and the right of a man not to have his good name sullied so that, whilst liability is strict in the sense that the defendant's intention is irrelevant, several defences are available.

LIBEL AND SLANDER

A defamatory statement or representation in permanent form is a libel, but if conveyed by spoken words or gestures, a slander. Apart from the written word, pictures, statues and waxwork effigies are libels. In addition, radio and television broadcasts are treated as publication in permanent form (Broadcasting Act 1990) as are words spoken during a theatrical performance (Theatres Act 1968).

Reading out a defamatory document to a third party is, on the balance of authority, a libel (*Forrester v. Tyrrell* (C.A., 1893)). To dictate defamatory material to a typist is clearly a slander, but if it is then put into a letter and sent to a third party the dictator publishes a libel through his agent. As far as defamatory matter on records and recorded tapes is concerned, there is a divergence of opinion among writers as to whether this is libel or potential slander.

An important distinction between libel and slander is that libel is actionable *per se*, without proof of special damage, whereas slander requires proof of such, except in the following cases. First, a direct imputation of a criminal offence punishable in the first instance with imprisonment (words conveying mere suspicion of the offence will not suffice). Secondly, an imputation that the plaintiff is presently suffering from a contagious or infectious disease likely to cause others to shun his society. Thirdly, an imputation of unchastity to any woman or girl (Slander of Women Act 1891). Fourthly, words calculated to disparage the plaintiff in any office, profession, calling, trade or business held or carried on by him at the time of the publication. The common law requirement that the words had to be spoken in the way of the plaintiff's calling has been removed by section 2 of the Defamation Act 1952. If, therefore, the natural tendency of the statement is to injure or prejudice the reputation of the plaintiff in his calling the words will be actionable *per se*.

Aside from these exceptions slander requires proof of special damage, which means loss of some temporal or material advantage such as loss of one's job or of the hospitality of one's friends (but mere exclusion from their society is not enough). The damage must not be too remote in accordance with general principles (see Chap. 4), although illness caused by mental anxiety induced by slander not actionable *per se* is considered too remote. Where a third party causes loss to the plaintiff as a result of the statement, that may or may not break the chain of causation depending upon what the defendant ought reasonably to have anticipated. Unauthorised repetition makes the damage too remote unless there is a legal or moral duty to repeat, or the defendant intends the repetition or if that is the natural and probable consequence of the original publication (*Speight v. Gosnay* (C.A., 1891); *Slipper v. British Broadcasting Corporation* (C.A., 1991)).

WHAT THE PLAINTIFF MUST PROVE

Whether the action is for libel or slander the plaintiff must prove that a defamatory statement referring to him was published.

Statement must be defamatory

The words must be defamatory in accordance with the definition already given, though it need not be proved that anyone who actually heard or read them believed them to be true. Where the statement tends to discredit the plaintiff only with a special class of persons, he may not succeed unless people generally would take the same view. In *Byrne v. Deane* (C.A., 1937), for example, it was held not to be defamatory to say of a club member that he had informed the police of an illicit gambling machine on the club premises, because right-thinking persons would not think less well of such a man. Problems may arise, however, where the general public is divided in its opinion. Thus, to say of another that he went to work during a strike would certainly lower him in the estimation of a considerable number of people and ought perhaps on that basis to be defamatory. The circumstances in which the statement is made may be important; words spoken at the height of a violent quarrel, for example, are not actionable if those who heard them understood them as mere abuse. The question in all cases is what interpretation the reasonable man would put upon the statement. In *Charleston v. News Group Newspapers Ltd* (H.L., 1995) the defendants published a potentially defamatory headline and photograph, but the text of the accompanying article plainly negated the defamatory meaning. The plaintiff was held to have no cause of action because, in the absence of a legal innuendo, the meaning to be ascribed to the words was the meaning which, taken as a whole, they conveyed to the ordinary, fair-minded reader, not to the limited category of those who only read headlines.

It is a question of law for the judge to decide whether the words are capable of a defamatory meaning and, if they are, it is for the jury to decide whether they are in fact. Whether the words are capable of bearing the defamatory meaning alleged by the plaintiff, or the meaning put forward by the defendant and contested by the plaintiff, may be tried as a preliminary issue (*Keays v. Murdoch Magazines (U.K.) Ltd* (C.A., 1991)). If the statement is plainly defamatory in its ordinary sense it is actionable (subject to any defence), unless the defendant can successfully explain away the defamatory meaning. Conversely, the words may be prima facie innocent but, in the light of extrinsic facts known to persons to whom the statement is published, bear some secondary defamatory meaning. This is a true, or legal, innuendo and is illustrated in *Tolley v. J. S. Fry & Sons Ltd* (H.L., 1931). The plaintiff, a well-known amateur golfer, was portrayed in an advertisement for the defendants' chocolate. He successfully pleaded an innuendo that he had received payment for his services and had thereby prostituted his amateur status. The extrinsic facts upon which the plaintiff relies in support of the innuendo must be known to the recipients of the statement at the time of publication and the plaintiff must, as a general rule, specify the persons whom he alleges to have knowledge of those facts (*Grappelli v. D. Block (Holdings) Ltd* (C.A., 1981)). It is plain from *Cassidy v. Daily Mirror Newspapers Ltd* (C.A., 1929) that it is immaterial that the defendant is unaware of the extrinsic facts.

Where the plaintiff does not rely upon extrinsic facts but merely contends that a particular meaning is to be attributed to the words themselves, there is said to be a "false" innuendo which, unlike the legal innuendo, does not give rise to a separate cause of action. In *Lewis v. Daily Telegraph Ltd* (H.L., 1964) the defendants published a statement that the fraud squad was investigating the plaintiffs' affairs. It was held that those words could not mean, as the plaintiffs alleged, that their affairs were conducted fraudulently, but simply meant that there was a suspicion of fraud, which the defendants admitted was prima facie defamatory but which they could justify.

Reference to the plaintiff

There must be a sufficient indication that the plaintiff is the subject of the statement, and in most cases, at least where the plaintiff is named, this presents no difficulty. The plaintiff need not be named, however, nor need there by any key or pointer in the statement to indicate him in particular, provided that people might reasonably draw the inference that it referred to him (*Morgan v. Odhams Press Ltd* (H.L., 1971)). Where a defamatory statement makes no reference to the plaintiff, he may rely on a later publication which clearly identifies him with the original statement (*Hayward v. Thompson* (C.A., 1982)).

It has long been the case that there is no requirement that the defendant must have intended to refer to the plaintiff (*Hulton & Co. v. Jones* (H.L., 1910)), and even if the statement is true of one person it may still be defamatory of another. Thus, in *Newstead v. London Express Newspaper Ltd* (C.A., 1940) the defendants were liable for their report that Harold Newstead, a 30-year-old Camberwell man, had been convicted of bigamy, which was true of X but untrue of the plaintiff, who bore the same name, was about the same age, and who also came from Camberwell.

In respect of a defamatory statement directed at a class of persons (*e.g.* doctors) no individual member of that class may usually sue unless there is some indication in the words, or the circumstances of their publication, which indicates a particular plaintiff. But if the reference is to a sufficiently limited class or group (*e.g.* the directors of a company) they may all be able to sue if it can be said that the words refer to each of them individually. These principles were established in *Knuppfer v. London Express Newspaper Ltd* (H.L., 1944).

Publication

There must be publication to at least one person other than the plaintiff or the defendant's spouse, but there is no publication by a typist or printer merely by handing the statement back to its author (*Eglantine Inn Ltd v. Smith* (H.C., 1948)). The defendant is liable if he intends further publication, for example by writing a letter to the correspondence editor of a newspaper (*Cutler v. McPhail* (H.C., 1962)). So, too, is he liable if he is negligent, as where he puts a letter in the wrong envelope or speaks too loudly in a crowded room. He is not liable if the statement is overheard by one whose presence is not to be expected, or if a letter is read by one who has no authority to do so (*Huth v. Huth* (C.A., 1915)). An unauthorised repetition or republication will break the chain of causation unless the statement is published to one who is under a legal or moral duty to repeat it, or the repetition is foreseeable as a natural and probable consequence of the original publication (*Speight v. Gosnay* (C.A., 1891); *Slipper v. British Broadcasting Corporation* (C.A., 1991)).

Every repetition of a defamatory statement is a fresh publication so that, as regards printed matter, the author, editor, printer and publisher are all liable. A mechanical distributor of print, such as a library or newsagent, is presumptively liable but will have a defence if he can prove that he did not know the work contained a libel, and that that lack of knowledge was not due to negligence in the conduct of his business (*Vizetelly v. Mudie's Select Library Ltd* (C.A., 1900)).

A person may be liable for failing to remove defamatory matter placed upon premises by a third party (*Byrne v. Deane* (C.A., 1937)). The extent of his duty to do so presumably depends upon whether he has control of the premises where the statement is displayed and the ease with which it can be removed.

DEFENCES

Unintentional defamation

Section 4 of the Defamation Act 1952 provides a defence where the statement is published innocently. The defendant may then make an offer of amends, which means an offer of a suitable correction and apology and, where copies of the statement have been distributed, an offer to take reasonable steps to notify recipients that the words are alleged to be defamatory. The offer must be made as soon as practicable after receipt by the defendant of notice that the words are or might be defamatory of the plaintiff, and if it is accepted and duly performed no proceedings may then be taken or continued, but if it is not, the defendant may plead it as a defence provided he published "innocently," and provided he can prove that, if he was not the author, the words were written by the author without malice. Publication is only innocent if either he did not intend to publish the statement about the plaintiff and he did not know of circumstances by virtue of which others might understand it to refer to him; or the statement was not prima facie defamatory and he did not

know of circumstances by virtue of which it might be understood
to be defamatory of the plaintiff. In either case the defendant
must have exercised all reasonable care in relation to the publication, so it is unlikely that the defence, even had it been
available at the time, would have succeeded in the *Newstead* case
(see above).

Justification

Justification or truth is generally an absolute defence, though the
defendant has the onus of proving the truth of the statement. He
need only show that the statement is substantially true and
whether the defence is lost through a minor inaccuracy is a
matter for the jury. Furthermore, section 5 of the Defamation
Act 1952 provides that the defence does not fail if the truth of
a number of charges cannot be proved, provided that the words
not proved to be true do not materially injure the palintiff's
reputation having regard to the truth of the remaining charges.
In such a case, the cautious plaintiff will plead only the untrue
allegation because the defendant cannot then rely on the publication as a whole and will presumably fail to justify. But, if the
plaintiff seeks to adopt this approach, the allegations must be
distinct (which is a question of fact and degree) and, if a number
of allegations taken together have a common "sting," the defendant is entitled to justify that sting (*Polly Peck (Holdings) plc v.
Trelford* (C.A., 1986)). If the defendant seeks to justify the repetition of a defamatory statement made to him he must, as a
general rule, prove that the statement is true and cannot simply
rely on the fact that another made it (*"Truth" (N.Z.) Ltd v.
Holloway* (P.C., 1960)). However, while hearsay and rumour
cannot constitute justification for what amounts to an assertion
of fact that the rumour is well founded, there may be circumstances in which the existence of a rumour entitles a person to
repeat it and to plead in justification that such a rumour is
in fact abroad (*Aspro Travel Ltd v. Owners Abroad Group plc* (C.A.,
1995)).

Where the defendant's allegation is that the plaintiff has been
convicted of an offence, section 13 of the Civil Evidence Act
1968 provides that proof that he stands convicted of it is conclusive evidence that he did commit it. The fact that the plaintiff's
conviction is "spent" under the Rehabilitation of Offenders
Act 1974 does not prevent the defendant from relying upon
justification, but in this case the defence is defeated by proof of
malice.

Fair comment

It is a defence that the statement is a fair comment upon a matter of public interest. What is in the public interest is a question of law for the judge and, whilst there is no exhaustive category of such matters, it covers the conduct of government and public institutions, works of art and literature produced for public consumption, theatrical productions and the like. A man's private life is not a matter of public interest unless it reflects upon his ability or fitness for public office.

The comment must be an honest expression of opinion based upon true facts existing at the time the comment was made, though the defence is still available where the comment is based upon an untrue statement made by another on a privileged occasion, provided that the defendant can also prove that he gave a fair and accurate report of the occasion on which the privileged statement was made (*Brent Walker Group plc v. Time Out Ltd* (C.A., 1991)). If the statement is one of fact rather than opinion the appropriate defence is justification. The facts upon which the comment is based need not be expressly stated but may be impliedly indicated in the circumstances of the publication (*Kemsley v. Foot* (H.L., 1952)). As far as the factual basis for the comment is concerned, the defence does not fail merely because the truth of every allegation of fact is not proved, as long as the expression of opinion is fair comment "having regard to such of the facts alleged or referred to in the words complained of as are proved" (Defamation Act 1952, s.6).

The comment must be fair and the test is whether the defendant was "an honest man expressing his genuine opinion" (Lord Denning M.R. in *Slim v. Daily Telegraph Ltd* (C.A., 1968)), though if the factual basis for the comment is untrue the defence fails, no matter how honest the defendant was. It is not for the defendant to prove that the comment was an honest expression of his own views but merely that it was objectively fair (*Telnikoff v. Matusevitch* (H.L., 1991)). However, although violent or exaggerated language does not make the comment unfair, if the plaintiff is charged with base or dishonest motives the defendant must prove that the comment is warranted by the facts in the sense that a fair-minded man might, in the light of those facts, bona fide hold such an opinion. (*Peter Walker Ltd v. Hodgson* (C.A., 1909)). Comment will not be fair if the defendant is actuated by malice in the sense of improper or evil motive, even though it would have been fair if made by one who genuinely believed it to be true (*Thomas v. Bradbury Agnew & Co. Ltd* (C.A.,1906)). With regard to the defence of qualified privilege (see later) malice on the part of one co-publisher will not "taint" another, and there is support for the view that the same rule applies to fair comment (*Lyon v. Daily Telegraph Ltd.* (C.A., 1943); *Telnikoff v. Matusevitch* (H.L., 1991)). The burden of proving malice rests upon the plaintiff (*Telnikoff v. Matusevitch* (H.L., 1991)).

Absolute privilege

Statements made on an occasion of absolute privilege are not actionable regardless of whether the defendant was malicious. They include the following:

(a) Statements made in the course of parliamentary proceedings including reports and papers ordered to be published by either House.

(b) Statements made during the course of judicial proceedings, whether by judge, jury, counsel or witnesses, provided they are broadly relevant to the issue before the court. The privilege extends not only to proceedings in an ordinary court of law but to any tribunal recognised by law and acting in a similar manner, even though it is not empowered to take a final decision on the issue (*Trapp v. Mackie* (H.L., 1979)). This was held in *Addis v. Crocker* (H.C., 1961) to include the Disciplinary Committee of the Law Society.

(c) Communications between solicitor and client in connection with litigation. It is not clear whether other communications attract absolute or merely qualified privilege, but in any event what passes between them is only protected in so far as it is reasonably referable to the solicitor-client relationship (*Minter v. Priest* (H.L., 1930)).

(d) Communications by one officer of state to another in the course of his official duty (*Chatterton v. Secretary of State for India* (C.A., 1895)). It is doubtful whether the privilege extends below communications on a ministerial level, though there may well be a qualified privilege.

(e) Fair and accurate reports in any newspaper (published at intervals not exceeding 26 days) or broadcast from a station, of public judicial proceedings in the United Kingdom (Law of Libel Amendment Act 1888; Defamation Act 1952, as amended by the Broadcasting Act 1990). The report must be published contemporaneously with the proceedings.

(f) Statutory protection is given to various reports of the Parliamentary Commissioner for Administration and of Local Commissioners.

Qualified privilege

This defence exists in respect of statements made for the protection of one's private interests or for the protection of the public interest, as where a complaint is laid before the proper authorities to secure the redress of a public grievance. It is also available where the maker of the statement and the recipient have a common interest in the matter, or where the recipient alone has an interest and the maker is under a legal, moral or social duty to communicate as, for instance, where a reference is given to a prospective employer. The common thread in all of these instances is that the defendant has either an interest in making, or a duty (legal, social or moral) to make the statement. But an equally essential requirement is that the person to whom the statement is made must either have a reciprocal interest or be under a corresponding duty to receive it (*Adam v. Ward* (H.L., 1917)).

An illustration of these principles is *Watt v. Longsdon* (C.A., 1930). The defendant director of a company received a letter from X, a manager of the company, which was defamatory of the plaintiff, who was managing director. The defendant replied to X in terms defamatory of the plaintiff and he also published X's letter to the company chairman and to the plaintiff's wife. In a libel action against the defendant it was held that his letter to X was privileged because both had a common interest in the company's affairs. The communication of X's letter to the chairman was also privileged on the grounds that the defendant was under a duty to report the matter. However, the defendant was held to be under no duty to communicate the letter to the plaintiff's wife, notwithstanding the obvious interest which she had in receiving it.

Whether or not there is a duty to communicate is a matter of law for the judge and no satisfactory test has evolved. In relation to the press it has been said that there is no defence of "fair information on a matter of public interest" and there is no duty to report that which is based on mere suspicion or conjecture (*Blackshaw v. Lord* (C.A., 1984)).

In addition to the above a number of reports are protected, including fair and accurate reports of parliamentary proceedings and of public judicial proceedings. The common law privilege in relation to the latter is wider than the statutory absolute privilege in that it applies to any form of publication made at any time. A number of fair and accurate reports published in newspapers or broadcast from a station in the United Kingdom receive qualified privilege by section 7 of the Defamation Act 1952. The reports so protected are to be found in the Schedule to the Act and are divided into two categories, those in the first being privileged "without explanation or contradiction," and those in the second "subject to explanation or contradiction." The defence is lost as regards those in the second category if the plaintiff requests the defendant to publish a reasonable statement by way of explanation or contradiction and the defendant refuses or neglects to do so. This statutory privilege does not extend to the publication of any matter which is not of public concern and the publication of which is not for the public benefit (section 7(3)). Whether the report is "fair and accurate" and the question of "public concern" and "public benefit," should be left to the jury (*Kingshott v. Associated Kent Newspapers Ltd* (C.A., 1991)).

Qualified privilege may be lost if the defendant publishes the statement more widely than is necessary for the protection of an interest. However, a publication by the defendant to third persons who have no interest or duty is nevertheless protected if it is reasonable and in the ordinary course of business. If, for example, X sends to Y a letter defamatory of Y which he first dictates to his secretary in the ordinary course of business, Y cannot sue for the publication to the secretary provided that the letter is written to protect or further the aims of the business (*Bryanston Finance Ltd v. de Vries* (C.A., 1975)).

The defence is also lost upon proof that the defendant was actuated by malice which may either mean lack of honest belief in the truth of the statement or use of the privilege for an improper purpose. Irrational prejudice or gross or exaggerated language does not amount to malice if the defendant's belief is honest (*Horrocks v. Lowe* (H.L., 1975)). His honesty is irrelevant, however, if he makes use of the occasion for an improper purpose as, for instance, where his aim is to spite rather than protect a legitimate interest. Where a defamatory statement is published by an agent on an occasion of privilege, malice on the part of the principal does not affect the agent's protection (*Egger v. Viscount Chelmsford* (C.A., 1965)). But if an employee maliciously publishes on a privileged occasion, the employer may be vicariously liable (*Riddick v. Thames Board Mills* (C.A., 1977)).

Apology

There is a defence under the Libel Act 1843 for a newspaper which publishes a libel without malice or gross negligence, which enables the defendant to publish a full apology and make a payment into court by way of amends. In practice, however, the defence has, for procedural reasons, fallen into disuse. A genuine apology may, however, go in mitigation of damages and its absence may aggravate them.

FUTURE REFORM

Apart from certain recent statutory and judicial changes governing damages in defamation, a Working Group under the chairmanship of Neill L.J. has made a number of proposals for changes, largely procedural, which the government has said it will implement. One proposal worthy of note is that the defence under section 4 of the Defamation Act 1952 should be more wide ranging in that the concept of "innocent publication" would protect the defendant unless the plaintiff could prove that he knew or was reckless as to three matters; namely, that the statement referred to the plaintiff or some identifiable person, that it was defamatory, and that it was false. Furthermore, there would be no need to show that the author was not actuated by malice. The requirement of an offer to publish a suitable correction and apology would remain, but the offer would include a statement indicating the defendant's willingness to pay such damages as might be determined by a judge.

---

11. NUISANCE

For the purposes of an action in tort a nuisance may be either private or public. In addition, there is a large number of statutory provisions aimed at the control of conduct which is damaging to the environment, some of which impose civil liability in respect of certain hazards. Enforcement of these provisions is in the hands of public bodies, which means that the plaintiff may save a good deal of time and expense by directing his complaint to the relevant body.

PRIVATE NUISANCE

The plaintiff may bring an action in private nuisance where the defendant unlawfully interferes with his use or enjoyment of his land or of some right (such as an easement) that he may have in relation to it. However, where the action is for interference with a servitude the plaintiff need only show a substantial degree of interference, and the defendant's conduct is then generally irrelevant so that no account is taken of those factors which may ordinarily assist in determining whether the defendant's user of land is reasonable (see later). What the plaintiff usually complains of is that there has been an "invasion" of his land as a result of some activity which the defendant has conducted upon his own land. Such activity is often not of itself unlawful, but it becomes a nuisance when the consequences of pursuing it extend to the land of his neighbour. Thus, to cause an encroachment upon the plaintiff's land of some tangible thing such as tree roots may be actionable (*Davey v. Harrow Corp.* (C.A., 1958)). The distinction between this form of invasion and a trespass is that, in this case, the interference is indirect. Causing physical damage to the land, or to the buildings or vegetation upon it, may constitute a nuisance, as where a drain becomes blocked and floods the plaintiff's land (*Sedleigh-Denfield v. O'Callaghan* (H.L., 1940)), or a building is allowed to fall into disrepair with the result that parts of it fall on the plaintiff's land (*Wringe v. Cohen* (C.A., 1940)). In these cases the interference is evidenced by tangible, physical damage, but it may equally be a nuisance merely to interfere with a neighbour's right to have quiet and comfortable enjoyment of his land. This may take a variety of forms, such as creating stench, dust, smoke, noise, vibration and, in *Thompson-Schwab v. Costaki* (C.A., 1956) the use of a house in a respectable, residential area for prostitution was held to be actionable (see also *Laws v. Florinplace* (II.C., 1981)).

Where the alleged nuisance produces material injury to property, the plaintiff will usually have little difficulty in proving that there has been an unlawful interference with his rights. But if the plaintiff's only complaint is that he cannot enjoy the use of his land to the full, he must prove a substantial interference with the comfort or convenience of living such as would adversely affect the average man. The law must seek to achieve a balance between two competing interests, namely that of the defendant to use his land as he wishes and that of his neighbour not to be seriously inconvenienced by his activities.

Not every interference is actionable, therefore, because people must be expected to tolerate a certain degree of noise or smell in the interests of peaceful co-existence. The interference only becomes unlawful when it is unreasonable.

Unreasonable interference

"The very essence of a private nuisance ... is the unreasonable use by a man of his land to the detriment of his neighbour" (Lord Denning M.R. in *Miller v. Jackson* (C.A., 1977)). The defendant's actual or constructive knowledge of that detriment is a factor in determining whether the interference is unreasonable, but a number of other factors, including the character and duration of the interference, must also be considered. Whether the defendant has unreasonably used his land cannot be gauged solely by reference to the nature of his conduct, because some foreseeable harm may be done which the law does not regard as excessive between neighbours under a principle of "give and take, or live and let live" (*Kennaway v. Thompson* (C.A., 1980)). In deciding the issue of reasonable user, the court may have regard to the following matters.

1. Degree of interference

Where physical damage to property has been done, a relatively small interference may amount to a nuisance, but in other cases the interference must be substantial, something more than ordinary everyday inconveniences, such as the plaintiff will be expected to put up with. In *Walter v. Selfe* (H.C., 1851) the test was said to be whether there was "an inconvenience materially interfering with the ordinary comfort physically of human existence, not merely according to elegant or dainty modes and habits of living, but according to plain and sober and simple notions among the English people." It is therefore a question of degree as to whether the interference is sufficiently serious, and a good illustration is *Halsey v. Esso Petroleum Co. Ltd* (H.C., 1961) where the defendants were held liable for, *inter alia*, nuisance caused by a nauseating smell emanating from their factory and by the noise at night both from the plant at their depot and from the arrival and departure of petrol tankers.

2. Nature of the locality

A person living in an industrial town cannot expect the same freedom from noise and pollution as one who lives in the country, but this is not a relevant consideration where there is physical injury to property. In *St. Helen's Smelting Co. v. Tipping* (H.L., 1865) the defendants were held liable for the emission of fumes from their factory in a manufacturing area which proved injurious to the plaintiff's shrubs. A grant of planning permission is not a licence to commit a nuisance, but where the effect of such is to alter the character of the neighbourhood, the question of whether a nuisance arises must be decided by reference to that character as altered and not as it was previously (*Gillingham Borough Council v. Medway (Chatham) Dock Co. Ltd* (H.C., 1992)). On the other hand, if the effect of the grant can not be regarded as changing the character of the neighbourhood, there may be an actionable nuisance even though the interference inevitably results from the authorised use (*Wheeler v. J. J. Saunders Ltd* (C.A., 1995)).

3. Social utility

The mere fact that the defendant's act is of benefit to the community will not in itself relieve the defendant of liability. Since nuisance is concerned with a balancing of conflicting interests, however, it may be that the plaintiff will have to bear minor disturbances. Once again it is a question of degree and if there is physical damage or the interference is substantial, the public interest should not be allowed to prevail over private rights (*Kennaway v. Thompson*(C.A., 1981); *cf. Miller v. Jackson* (C.A., 1977)). In *Adams v. Ursell* (H.C., 1913) the smell from a fried-fish shop was held to constitute a nuisance to nearby residents, notwithstanding the defendant's argument that he was providing a valuable service to poor people in the neighbourhood.

4. Abnormal sensitivity

A man cannot increase the liabilities of his neighbour by applying his own property to special uses, whether for business or for pleasure (*Eastern and South African Telegraph Co. Ltd v. Cape Town Tramways Co. Ltd* (P.C., 1902)). Thus, in *Robinson v. Kilvert* (C.A., 1889) warm air from the defendant's premises increased the temperature in an upper part of the building and caused damage to stocks of brown paper which the plaintiff stored there. The amount of heat was not such as to cause annoyance or inconvenience to those working for the plaintiff, nor was it harmful to paper generally, so the action failed. The same principle applies to sensitive persons, and no regard is had to the particular needs of individuals such as those with an acute sense of smell or hearing (*Heath v. Brighton Corp.* (H.C., 1908)) Once a nuisance is established, however, the plaintiff can recover even in respect of delicate operations, such as the cultivation of orchids (*McKinnon Industries Ltd v. Walker* (P.C., 1951)). It was doubted in *Bridlington Relay Ltd v. Y.E.B.* (H.C., 1965) whether the reception of television signals by a householder was a use of land which the law would protect but this must be regarded as suspect at the present day.

5. State of affairs

It is often said that the interference must be continuous or recurrent rather than merely temporary or occasional. An injunction will not normally be granted unless there is some degree of permanence in the defendant's activities, except in extreme cases (see, *e.g. De*

Keyser's Royal Hotel Ltd v. Spicer Bros. Ltd (H.C., 1914)). Where the plaintiff claims damages the duration of the interference, and the times at which it occurs, are important in determining whether the defendant is liable. A man who builds an extension on to the back of his house no doubt causes inconvenience to his neighbour, but he is not liable for nuisance if he takes all reasonable care to see that no undue annoyance is caused (*Harrison v. Southwark and Vauxhall Water Co.* (H.C., 1891)). If, on the other hand, he conducts his operations at unreasonable hours, or takes an inordinately long time, or uses antiquated methods and thereby increases the level of interference, he may be liable (*Andreae v. Selfridge & Co. Ltd* (C.A., 1938)).

An isolated escape is probably not actionable as a nuisance (*S.C.M. (United Kingdom) Ltd v. Whittall & Son Ltd* (H.C., 1970)), though it may afford evidence of the existence of a dangerous state of affairs upon the defendant's land. In *Spicer v. Smee* (H.C., 1946), for example, defective electrical wiring which started a fire and caused damage to adjacent property was held to constitute a nuisance. Furthermore, there may be liability in negligence or under the rule in *Rylands v. Fletcher* (see Chap. 12) in respect of a single escape.

6. Intentional annoyance

If the defendant prosecutes his activity with the express purpose of annoying his neighbour, he will be liable, even though the degree of interference would not constitute a nuisance if done in the ordinary and reasonable use of property (*Christie v. Davey* (H.C., 1893)). Thus, in *Hollywood Silver Fox Farm Ltd v. Emmett* (H.C., 1936) the defendant deliberately fired his gun near the boundary of the plaintiff's land in order to disturb the breeding of the plaintiff's silver foxes. Many of the vixens aborted, for which damage the defendant was held liable. An anomalous case is *Bradford Corp. v. Pickles* (H.L., 1895) where, in order to induce the plaintiffs to buy his land, the defendant abstracted percolating water, which flowed in undefined channels beneath his land and which fed the plaintiffs' reservoir. His motive was held to be irrelevant and he was therefore not liable. This is distinguishable from *Emmett* on the ground that the plaintiff had no right to receive the water, so that there was no interest to be protected. The right to make noise on one's land, however, is qualified by the right of one's neighbour to the quiet enjoyment of his land. A landowner's right to abstract subterranean water flowing in undefined channels, regardless of the consequences to his neighbour and of his motive, was affirmed in *Stephens v. Anglian Water Authority* (C.A., 1987).

Damage

Damage must usually be proved, either in the form of tangible injury to land or to property upon it, or in the form of substantial personal discomfort, though nuisance to a servitude may be actionable *per se*. It is not clear whether damages for personal injury are recoverable in private nuisance but, if they are, it is likely that the plaintiff would only succeed upon proof of negligence. If nuisance were to offer a stricter form of liability in such a case the person with a proprietary interest in the land affected would be in a better position than, for example, members of the same household without any such interest (see later). It may be that where the interference culminates in personal injury the claim should be brought in negligence (see, *e.g. Cunard v. Antifyre Ltd* (H.C., 1933)).

Who can sue

It was once the rule that only a person with an interest in the land affected could maintain an action in private nuisance so that a mere licensee, such as a hotel guest or lodger, could not (*Malone v. Laskey* (C.A., 1907)). It may be, however, that a person without any such interest can sue, if to deny a right of action would cause manifest injustice. Thus, in *Khorasandjian v. Bush* (C.A., 1993) a majority upheld the grant of an injunction to an occupier's daughter to restrain a private nuisance in the form of persistent, harassing telephone calls (see also Chap. 1).

A landlord out of possession cannot sue unless he can show a likelihood of permanent damage to his reversionary interest. Where there is a continuing nuisance the owner or occupier can recover even though the damage occurs before he acquires his interest and he is aware of it (*Masters v. Brent London Borough Council* (H.C., 1978)).

Who is liable

1. The creator

The creator of the nuisance is liable whether or not he occupies the land whence the interference emanates (*Hall v. Beckenham Corp.* (H.C., 1949)). He remains liable even if he parts with possession and is no longer able to stop the nuisance without committing trespass.

2. The occupier

The occupier will be liable if he creates the nuisance, but, apart from this, he may incur liability either in respect of the acts of others upon his land or where the nuisance existed before he became the occupier. He may, for example, be answerable for those whom he allows on to his land as guests (*Att.-Gen. v. Stone* (H.C., 1895)), at least if he knew or should have known of the interference. Although the general rule is that an employer is not liable for the defaults of his contractor, he will be liable if he is under a non-delegable duty, as where there is a withdrawal of support from neighbouring land (*Bower v. Peate* (H.C., 1876)), or operations are conducted on or adjoining the highway (*Tarry v. Ashton* (H.C., 1876); see Chap. 14). It seems that he will also be liable whenever the work that the contractor is employed to do creates a foreseeable risk of nuisance. In *Matania v. National Provincial Bank Ltd* (C.A., 1936) the occupier of premises who employed contractors to carry out alterations was held liable for nuisance by dust and noise caused to other occupants in the building. In *Spicer v. Smee* (H.C., 1946) it was said that "where danger is likely to arise unless the work is properly done, there is a duty to see that it is properly done," but this proposition is probably too wide (*Salsbury v. Woodland* (C.A., 1970)).

If a nuisance is created by a trespasser, the occupier is liable not only if he adopts the nuisance for his own purposes (*Page Motors Ltd v. Epsom and Ewell B.C.*(H.C., 1982)) but also if, with actual or constructive knowledge of its existence, he fails to take reasonable steps to abate it (in which case he is said to "continue" the nuisance). This principle was laid down in *Sedleigh-Denfield v. O'Callaghan* (H.L., 1940) and has since been extended to dangerous states of affairs which arise naturally upon the land. In *Goldman v. Hargrave* (P.C., 1967) a tree on the defendant's land was struck by lightning and caught fire. The defendant had the tree felled and decided to let the fire burn itself out, but it eventually spread to and damaged the plaintiff's land. The defendant was held liable because, with actual knowledge of the danger, he failed to take reasonable steps to abate it (followed in *Leakey v. National Trust* (C.A., 1980)); however, it was held in *Home Brewery Co. Ltd v. William Davis & Co. (Leicester) Ltd*(H.C., 1987) that a lower occupier cannot sue a higher occupier for permitting the natural flow of water to pass to the lower ground, but that the lower occupier can erect barriers to prevent the flow provided that, in so doing, he does not put his land to an unreasonable use. In this type of case liability is based essentially upon proof of negligence with one important difference, namely that, since the danger is not of the occupier's own making, his individual circumstances should be taken into account, including his financial resources. The test of reasonableness therefore imports a subjective element. As far as the encroachment of tree roots is concerned, liability was imposed without qualification in *Davey v. Harrow Corporation* (C.A., 1958). This was approved in *Leakey's* case subject to the proviso that actual or constructive knowledge of the defect was required in accordance with the *Goldman* formula, and it is now clear from *Solloway v. Hampshire C.C.* (C.A., 1981) that the defendant is only liable if there was a foreseeable risk of damage by encroachment which he could reasonably be expected to take steps to guard against.

Where a nuisance has been created by the occupier's predecessor the plaintiff must prove that he knew, or ought to have known, of its existence (*St. Anne's Well Brewery Co. v. Roberts* (C.A., 1928)).

3. The landlord

Where the premises are let the usual person to sue is the tenant. The landlord will, however, be liable in the following circumstances. First, if he expressly or impliedly authorises the nuisance, as where the interference arises as a result of using the land for the very purpose for which it was let (*Harris v. James* (H.C., 1876); *Tetley v. Chitty* (H.C., 1986)). In *Smith v. Scott* (H.C., 1973) a local authority was held not to have authorised the commission of a nuisance by a "problem" family which it had housed next to the plaintiff. Secondly, he is liable if he either knew or ought to have known of the nuisance before letting the premises. Thirdly, if the premises fall into disrepair during the period of the lease, he is liable if he has reserved the right to enter and repair (*Heap v. Ind Coope & Allsopp Ltd* (C.A., 1940)), and such a right will readily be implied in a short-term tenancy (*Mint v. Good* (C.A., 1951); but the significance of this decision is greatly reduced by the Landlord and Tenant Act 1985 which provides that, where a dwelling-house is let for less than seven years, there is an implied covenant by the landlord to keep in repair the structure and exterior of the premises, and certain installations for the supply of essential services). The landlord is clearly liable where he is under an express covenant to repair, but it was held in *Brew Bros. Ltd v. Snax (Ross) Ltd* (C.A., 1970) that he does not escape responsibility by extracting that obligation from his tenants, provided that he knows or ought to know of the nuisance. In one particular case, that is where premises adjoining a highway collapse and cause injury to a passer-by or to an adjoining owner, liability is, according to *Wringe v. Cohen* (C.A., 1940) strict, subject to a defence either that the defect was due to a secret and unobservable process of nature or to the act of a trespasser (but in the latter case see *Sedleigh-Denfield v. O'Callaghan* (above)).

Apart from these common law obligations the landlord may also be liable under the Defective Premises Act 1972, s.4. This provides that if the landlord is under an obligation to his tenant to repair, or has an express or implied power to enter and repair, he owes a duty to take reasonable care to see that all who might reasonably be expected to be affected by defects in the state of the premises are reasonably safe from personal injury or damage to their property. A right to repair will be implied where the landlord could, if necessary, obtain an injunction to enter and effect repairs (*McAuley v. Bristol City Council* (C.A., 1992)).

Defences

1. Prescription

A right to commit a private nuisance may be acquired by 20 years' continuance thereof, though it may be that this is only so where the right is capable of existing as an easement. It has been doubted whether the defendant can acquire a prescriptive right to cause unlawful interference by such things as noise, smoke, smell or vibration in which the degree of inconvenience is variable and may at times cease altogether. The plaintiff must have full knowledge of the nuisance before the period begins to run, and there must have been an actionable nuisance during the 20 years. In *Sturges v. Bridgman* (C.A., 1879) the plaintiff built a consulting room at the end of his garden and complained of noise from the defendant's premises. The defendant's argument that he had been pursuing his trade for more than 20 years failed, because the interference did not become actionable as a nuisance until the plaintiff extended his premises.

2. Statutory authority

Many nuisance actions arise out of the activities of bodies authorised by statute to conduct those operations. It is generally a defence to prove that the interference is an inevitable result of what they were obliged or empowered to do, so that there will be no liability without negligence (*Manchester Corporation v. Farnworth* (H.L., 1930)). The following principles were laid down in *Department of Transport v. North West Water Authority* (H.L., 1984). First, in fulfilling a statutory duty there is no liability without negligence, whether or not liability for nuisance is expressly preserved in the

Act. Secondly, in exercising a statutory power, liability depends upon whether nuisance is expressly preserved; if it is, negligence need not be proved, but if it is not, there is no liability in the absence of negligence (see also Chap. 12).

Precisely what a body is authorised or obliged to do depends upon the provisions of the Act. A liberal interpretation was given in *Allen v. Gulf Oil Refining Ltd* (H.L., 1981) where authority to acquire land and build a refinery was held to confer, by necessary implication, the right to operate the refinery. Since there was no express provision for liability in nuisance, the defendants were held not liable for the inevitable consequences of working the refinery.

3. Coming to nuisance

It is no defence that the plaintiff moved into the area of the nuisance (*Miller v. Jackson* (C.A., 1977)).

4. Other defences

Consent and contributory negligence are valid defences, although not likely in nuisance actions. Necessity, act of God, and act of a stranger are defences provided that there is no negligence. It is no defence, however, that the nuisance was the product of the combined acts of two or more persons, though the act of any one individual would not be unlawful (*Lambton v. Mellish* (H.C., 1894)).

Remedies

The plaintiff may recover damages for any resulting loss which is of a reasonably foreseeable kind (*The Wagon Mound (No. 2)* (P.C., 1967)).

The remedy of an injunction is an equitable one and will therefore only be granted where damages would be inadequate. If the interference is trivial or temporary it is unlikely to be granted, but it should not be refused simply on the ground that the defendant's activity is in the public interest. For the factors to be considered in determining whether damages should be awarded in lieu of an injunction see *Shelfer v. City of London Electric Lighting Co.* (C.A., 1895). The principles laid down in that case were applied in *Jaggard v. Sawyer* (C.A., 1995) where the fact that the defendants had acted openly and in good faith, and that the plaintiff had delayed in seeking interlocutory relief, were considered to be relevant (though not conclusive) factors in deciding that the grant of an injunction would be oppressive. The majority decision in *Miller v. Jackson* (C.A., 1977) not to grant an injunction in respect of the frequent escape of cricket balls from the defendant's land because the cricket club was a valuable local amenity, was held to be wrong in *Kennaway v. Thompson* (C.A., 1981). An injunction is a flexible remedy and terms may be imposed, for example as to the types of activity permitted and the times at which it may be conducted. This was done in *Kennaway* (above) but the court refused to do so in *Tetley v. Chitty* (H.C., 1986), distinguishing *Kennaway* on the ground that, in that case, the defendants had been pursuing their activities before the plaintiff moved into the area.

The standard of liability

A question of some considerable difficulty is the extent to which fault (*i.e.* negligence) is relevant to an action in nuisance. According to the House of Lords in *Cambridge Water Co. v. Eastern Counties Leather plc* (H.L., 1994), subject to the concept of reasonable user liability is generally regarded as strict; that is to say that if the defendant's user is unreasonable it matters not that he took all reasonable care to avoid the interference. This at least is the position where the defendant actively created the dangerous state of affairs which caused the damage; in other cases, as has been noted, the plaintiff will generally have to prove fault. A distinction must be drawn between a claim for damages and an application for an injunction to restrain future harm. In the latter case the defendant will inevitably become aware of the interference at the latest when the plaintiff institutes proceedings, so the question of fault is then largely irrelevant; the defendant's conduct is deliberate as soon as he has knowledge of the interference, and the court is simply concerned with whether the degree of interference exceeds that which the plaintiff can reasonably be expected to tolerate.

Where the defendant could not reasonably have foreseen the possibility of interference of the type which in fact occurs he is not liable. If he later acquires actual or constructive knowledge of a potential danger he may be liable in negligence if he fails to take steps to abate it, but he cannot it seems be liable once that danger has passed out of his control. What is not clear from *Cambridge Water* is the position where the defendant knows that his activity creates a possible risk and takes all reasonable care to avoid it. To suggest that the defendant would not be liable in the absence of fault seems to run counter to dicta in Lord Goff's judgment that the defendant would be strictly liable if the risk materialised. On the other hand it is not easy to see how the defendant can be said to have put his land to an unreasonable use for so long as the activity is conducted with reasonable care without causing any interference to his neighbours. It would appear that the question of the extent to which liability is truly strict therefore requires further elucidation.

PUBLIC NUISANCE

A public nuisance may be defined as an unlawful act or omission which materially affects the comfort and convenience of a class of Her Majesty's subjects who come within the sphere of its operation; whether the number of persons affected is sufficiently large to warrant the epithet "public" is a question of fact (*Att.-Gen. v. P.Y.A. Quarries Ltd* (C.A., 1957)). At common law, public nuisances cover a wide variety of activities such as carrying on an offensive trade, selling food unfit for human consumption and obstructing the highway.

Public and private nuisance

Public nuisance is a crime in respect of which the Attorney-General may, if a criminal prosecution is felt to be inadequate, bring a "relator" action for an injunction to restrain the offending activity.

The same conduct may amount to both a private and a public nuisance, but an individual may only sue in tort in respect of the latter if he has suffered "particular" damage, which means loss or damage over and above that suffered by the rest of the class affected. This encompasses personal injury, and there is clearly no requirement that the plaintiff must have an interest in the land (though see, too, *Khorasandjian v. Bush*, noted earlier in this Chap.). In *Halsey v. Esso Petroleum Co. Ltd* (H.C., 1961) the plaintiff's washing has damaged by the emission of acid smuts from the defendants' factory, as was the paintwork of his car which was parked in the road outside his house. The damage to the washing was actionable as a private nuisance, whilst that to the car amounted to particular damage for the purposes of an action in public nuisance. The term "particular damage" may also include loss of an economic nature consequential upon the interference. In *Tate & Lyle Industries Ltd v. G.L.C.* (H.L., 1983) the plaintiffs were held entitled to recover the cost of dredging to facilitate access to their jetty, which had been obstructed by the defendants' building works (see also *Lyons, Sons & Co. v. Gulliver*, below).

Nuisance on the highway

Perhaps the most common instance of public nuisance is an unlawful obstruction or interference with the public's right of passage along the highway. In *Castle v. St. Augustine's Links* (H.C., 1922), for example, the defendant golf club was held liable for so siting one of its fairways that golf balls were frequently sliced on to the highway, with the result that the plaintiff was injured while driving along the road when a ball crashed through the windscreen of his car.

In relation to obstructions, the defendant is liable only if he creates an unreasonable risk, but he is generally liable for the defaults of his contractor because of the non-delegable nature of the duty (see Chap. 14). If the obstruction is reasonable in terms of duration and degree, such as a van delivering goods to a shop, it is generally not actionable.

To conduct one's trade in such a manner as to cause a foreseeable obstruction is actionable, and if such obstruction causes loss of custom to other traders, that is special damage (*Lyons, Sons & Co. v. Gulliver* (C.A., 1914)). But the defendant is not liable for an obstruction, such as a queue outside his shop, which is beyond his control. The plaintiff must in all cases prove damage.

Where damage is done by a projection over the highway, there may be a distinction between artificial and natural things. In the case of the former, liability may be strict (*Tarry v. Ashton* (H.C., 1876)), whereas in the case of natural projections (for example, trees) it seems that negligence must be proved and, even though the source of the nuisance is plain to see, the occupier will not be liable until he has actual or constructive knowledge that it is a danger (*British Road Services Ltd v. Slater* (H.C., 1964)). With regard to premises adjoining the highway, the nature of the liability imposed by *Wringe v. Cohen* (C.A., 1940) has already been mentioned.

A highway authority is under a duty to maintain the highway and may be liable in negligence, nuisance or for breach of statutory duty under the Highways Act 1980. This right of action for non-repair does not, however, extend to claims for pure economic loss (*Wentworth v. Wiltshire County Council* (C.A., 1993)). The Act provides that it shall be a defence to prove that the authority had taken such care as in all the circumstances was reasonably required to make sure that the part of the highway to which the action relates was not dangerous for traffic. Apart from the statutory duty a highway authority may be under a common law duty, for example to take reasonable steps to remove dangers to road users caused by impaired visibility of which it was aware (*Stovin v. Wise* (C.A., 1994)).

12. STRICT LIABILITY

INTRODUCTION

Although the law of tort is predominantly fault based there are instances in which liability may be imposed without negligence on the defendant's part. Thus, there may be strict liability for damage caused by defective products (see Chap. 6) and animals (see Chap. 13), and an employer's vicarious liability for the torts of his employees is similarly not dependent on fault on the part of the employer (see Chap. 14). It has also been seen that liability in nuisance may be strict where the defendant created the source of the interference, in the sense that, if the defendant's user is unreasonable, it is irrelevant that he took all reasonable care to avoid it. Strict civil liability is also imposed by certain statutes; see, *e.g.* Nuclear Installations Act 1965.

Apart from the above instances a form of strict liability may arise under the rule in *Rylands v. Fletcher* (H.L., 1868) and in respect of the escape of fire. The incidence of such liability is the subject of this chapter.

The rule in Rylands v. Fletcher

Although the rule had its origins in nuisance it had, until recently, come to be regarded as having evolved into a distinct principle governing liability for the escape of dangerous things. However, in *Cambridge Water Co. Ltd v. Eastern Counties Leather plc* (H.L., 1994) it was said that it would lead to a more coherent body of common law principles if the rule were to be regarded as an extension of the law of nuisance to cases of isolated escapes from land (even though the rule is not limited to escapes which are in fact isolated). It is therefore doubtful whether the rule can still be considered as an independent species of liability, though its separate treatment may be justified on the ground that a number of issues were left undecided by the House of Lords in *Cambridge Water*.

The rule itself was stated by Blackburn J. as follows; "We think that the true rule of law is, that the person who for his own pur- poses brings on his lands and collects and keeps there anything likely to do mischief if it escapes must keep it in at his peril, and, if he does not do so, is prima facie answerable for all the damage which is the natural consequence of its escape." The House of

Lords added the qualification that the defendant must have put his land to a non-natural use.

Things brought on to the land

There is no liability for an escape of things naturally upon the land such as self-sown vegetation (*Giles v. Walker* (C.A., 1890)), or an outcrop of rock which falls by the process of weathering (*Pontardawe R.D.C. v. Moore-Gwyn* (H.C., 1929)). The defendant may however be liable in nuisance or negligence in accordance with *Goldman v. Hargrave* (see Chap. 11), and will also be liable if he is instrumental in causing the escape of something naturally upon his land, as where the blasting of explosives caused an escape of rock (*Miles v. Forest Rock Granite Co. Ltd* (C.A., 1918).

Likely to do mischief

The rule has over the years been applied to a wide variety of things including water, gas, electricity, fire, explosions, vibrations, noxious fumes, flag-poles and fairground swings. However, the House of Lords in *Cambridge Water* rejected any rationalisation of the rule into a broad principle of liability for damage caused by extra hazardous activities, inclining to the view that this was a matter best left to Parliament. It was also held that, by analogy with nuisance, the rule did not apply unless damage of the relevant type was foreseeable as the result of an escape, though it was made clear that liability was strict notwithstanding that the defendant had exercised all reasonable care and skill to prevent the escape.

Escape

There must be an "escape from a place where the defendant has occupation or control over land to a place which is outside his occupation or control" (*Read v. J. Lyons & Co. Ltd* (H.L., 1947). Provided there has been a non-natural user the thing which escapes need not be the subject-matter of the accumulation (*Miles v. Forest Rock Granite Co. Ltd* (C.A., 1918)).

The defendant need not have any interest in the land from which the thing escapes; in *Rigby v. Chief Constable of Northamptonshire* (H.C., 1985) it was considered that the rule applied where a dangerous thing was brought on to the highway whence it escaped and caused damage. Whether the plaintiff himself need be an occupier is unclear. An affirmative answer was given in *Weller v. Foot and Mouth Disease Research Institute* (H.C., 1966), and dicta in *Read v. Lyons* support that view, but there are a number of authorities to the contrary (see, *e.g. Shiffman v. Order of St. John* (H.C., 1936); *Perry v. Kendrick's Transport Ltd* (C.A., 1956)).

It is doubtful if the rule applies to the intentional projection of things on to the plaintiff's land. In this case trespass is the more appropriate cause of action (*Rigby v. Chief Constable of Northamptonshire*).

Non-natural user

It has already been noted that the defendant is not liable under the rule for an escape of something naturally upon the land. In *Cambridge Water* it was said that the concept of non-natural user limits liability under the rule just as the concept of reasonable user does in a nuisance action, though the relationship, if any, between the two was not discussed. It is however clear from that case that there is no liability for deliberate accumulations unless there has been a non-natural user by the defendant, which was defined in *Rickards v. Lothian* (P.C. 1913), in the following terms: "It must be some special use bringing with it increased danger to others, and must not merely be the ordinary use of land or such a use as is proper for the general benefit of the community."

A distinction must therefore be drawn between an "ordinary" and an "extraordinary" use of land, though the concept of non-natural user has enabled the courts to adopt a flexible approach and to adapt the application of the rule to changing circumstances of time and place (see *Read v. Lyons*, where there are dicta to the effect that a munitions factory in time of war was a normal use of land). In the past, domestic water supplies, household fires, electric wiring in houses and shops, the ordinary working of mines and minerals and the keeping of trees and shrubs (unless, perhaps, poisonous: *Crowhurst v. Amersham Burial Board* (Ex., 1878)) have been held to be natural uses. On the other hand the bulk storage of water, gas or electricity and the collection of sewage by a local authority have at various times been held non-natural. A more recent approach adopted in *Mason v. Levy Auto Parts of England Ltd* (H.C., 1967) was to equate the concept of non-natural user with that of abnormal risk, so that the court took account of the quantity of the accumulation of combustible material, the manner in which it was stored, and the character of the neighbourhood, and conceded that those considerations might equally have justified a finding of negligence.

Although, according to the original formulation of the rule, the defendant must have collected the thing "for his own purpose," this did not at one time necessarily mean that he should derive any personal benefit (*Smeaton v. Ilford Corporation* (H.C., 1954)). Where, however, the accumulation is for the public benefit pursuant, for example, to the provision of a public service (*Dunne v. North Western Gas Board* (C.A., 1964)) or indeed to ordinary manufacturing processes (*British Celanese Ltd v. A. H. Hunt (Capacitors) Ltd* (H.C., 1969)) the more modern tendency has been to deny the application of the rule.

The status of the above authorities will now have to be reconsidered in the light of *Cambridge Water*. In that case it was said that the storage of large quantities of chemicals on industrial premises was "an almost classic case of non-natural use" even in an industrial area. Furthermore, the fact that the chemical in question was commonly used in the particular industry, and that the defendants' operations served to support a local industrial community, was not sufficient to render the use natural. Unfortunately there was no real discussion of the relationship between public benefit and non-natural user, so the matter awaits further clarification.

Personal injury

It is unclear whether the plaintiff can succeed in a claim for personal injuries, and there was no discussion of this point in *Cambridge Water*. The view of Lord Macmillan in *Read v. Lyons* was that the plaintiff would have to prove negligence, at least if he is a non-occupier, but there is authority to the contrary (*Shiffman v. Order of St. John*; *Perry v. Kendrick's Transport Ltd* (see earlier in this chapter)). Insofar as liability under the rule is strict it would seem illogical to distinguish between an occupier and a non-occupier for this purpose, and thereby to place the former in a more advantageous position.

Remoteness of damage

Following *Cambridge Water* the test for remoteness would appear to be reasonable foreseeability, as it is in nuisance, although the case does not speak in terms of remoteness as such. Referring to the phrase "likely to do mischief if it escapes" taken from the original formulation of the rule it was said that the general tenor of the statement was that "knowledge, or at least foreseeability of the risk, is a prerequisite of the recovery of damages ... ". It is not entirely clear from this whether both the escape and the consequences thereof must be foreseeable or merely whether, given that an escape has occurred, the consequences alone must be foreseeable, though the actual decision seems to support the former analysis.

Defences

There are a number of defences, the first three of which mentioned below, together with the concept of non-natural user, have gone a long way towards introducing elements of fault into this area of the law.

1. Act of God

An act of God is an operation of natural forces "which no human foresight can provide against, and of which human prudence is not bound to recognise the possibility." But this is not to say that the defendant will escape liability merely because the event is not reasonably foreseeable. Two cases may be contrasted: in *Nichols v. Marsland* (C.A., 1876) the defendant was held not liable when an exceptionally violent rainfall caused his artificial ornamental lakes to flood his neighbour's land. This decision was criticised in *Greenock Corp. v. Caledonian Ry.* (H.L., 1917) where, on similar facts, the defendant was held liable on the ground that it is insufficient for him to show that the occurrence was one which could not reasonably be anticipated. He must go further and prove that no human foresight could have recognised the possibility of such an event. For practical purposes the defence is therefore of very limited application.

2. Act of a stranger

The defendant is not liable if the escape is due to the unforeseeable act of a third party over whom he has no control. In *Rickards v. Lothian* (P.C., 1913) the occupier of a lavatory was not liable when an unknown person deliberately blocked up the overflow pipe and caused flooding on the plaintiff's premises. The defence is not available, however, if the act is one which the defendant ought reasonably to have foreseen and guarded against. In *Northwestern Utilities Ltd. v. London Guarantee and Accident Co.* (P.C., 1936) the defendants' gas main was fractured by a local authority in the course of constructing a sewer. The defendants were held liable in negligence for damage caused by an explosion of the gas because they knew of the work being carried out and, in view of the risks involved, should have checked to make sure that no damage had been done to their mains. In cases such as this a claim based on *Rylands v. Fletcher* merges into a claim for negligence, though according to Goddard L.J. in *Hanson v. Wearmouth Coal Co.* (C.A., 1939) the onus is upon the defendant to prove both that the escape was caused by the independent act of a third party and that he could not reasonably have anticipated and guarded against it.

For the purposes of this defence a trespasser is a stranger but servants within the course of their employment and independent contractors are not. The defendant is probably responsible for the acts of his family and guests, although the issue is not entirely free from doubt and may depend upon the degree of control which he can be expected to exercise over them. In *Hale v. Jennings Bros.* (C.A., 1938) the defendant was held liable for the deliberate act of a lawful visitor in tampering with a potentially dangerous machine.

3. Consent of the plaintiff

Express or implied consent to the presence of the dangerous thing is a defence unless the defendant was negligent (*Att.-Gen. v. Cory Bros. & Co. Ltd.* (H.L., 1921)). Consent may be implied where a thing is brought on to the land for the common benefit of the plaintiff and defendant as, for example, where one cistern supplies water to several flats. A further aspect of implied consent is that a person who enters into occupation of property as a tenant takes it as he finds it in so far as he knows of the presence of the dangerous thing (*Peters v. Prince of Wales Theatre (Birmingham) Ltd.* (C.A., 1943)). In *Northwestern Utilities Ltd. v. London Guarantee & Accident Co. Ltd.* (P.C., 1936) the issue of common benefit was held not to be relevant as between the consumer of a product such as gas or electricity, and the supplier and, notwithstanding dicta in *Dunne v. North Western Gas Board* (C.A., 1964) to the contrary, such a view would seem to accord with *Cambridge Water*.

4. Default of the plaintiff

If the plaintiff's own act or default causes the damage no action will lie. In *Dunn v. Birmingham Canal Navigation Co.* (E.C., 1872) the plaintiffs persisted in working their mine beneath the defendant's canal and failed in their action when water flooded the mine. Where the plaintiff is partly at fault the defence of contributory negligence will apply.

If damage is caused only by reason of the extra-sensitive nature of the plaintiff's property he may not, by analogy with nuisance (see Chap. 11), be able to recover (*Eastern and South African Telegraph Co. Ltd. v. Cape Town Tramways Co. Ltd.* (P.C., 1902)). However, in *Hoare & Co. v. McAlpine* (H.C., 1923) it was thought not to be a good defence that a building damaged by vibrations was exceptionally unstable.

5. Statutory authority

This may afford a defence as in nuisance and the same principles of law apply (see Chap. 11).

THE ESCAPE OF FIRE

Common law

At common law a person was liable if a fire spread from his premises and did damage to adjoining premises, though there is some doubt as to whether or not liability was strict. He is now liable where the fire is caused by negligence or nuisance, or where it starts or spreads as a result of a non-natural user of land, in which case negligence need not be proved. The latter instance is simply an application of the rule in *Rylands v. Fletcher* except that it is not the thing accumulated that escapes, and the test, according to *Mason v. Levy Auto Parts of England Ltd.* (H.C., 1967) is whether the defendant brought to his land things likely to catch fire and kept them there in such conditions that if they did ignite the fire would be likely to spread. Although liability under *Rylands v. Fletcher* is supposedly strict there seems to be little difference between this formulation and ordinary negligence.

There is a defence in respect of a fire started by an act of God or a stranger, though the defendant may be under a duty to abate a known danger upon his land in accordance with the principle in *Goldman v. Hargrave* (P.C., 1967). The term "stranger" applies only to those over whom the defendant has no control, so that there is liability for fires started by the default of a servant (*Musgrove v. Pandelis* (C.A., 1919)), an independent contractor (*Balfour v. Barty-King* (C.A., 1957)), a guest (*Crogate v. Morris* (1617)) and perhaps any person lawfully upon his land whom he has authorised or permitted to start a fire (*H. & N. Emanuel v. GLC* (C.A., 1971)).

Statute

The Fires Prevention (Metropolis) Act 1774 provides that no action shall lie against a person upon whose land a fire accidentally begins. This provision only applies to fires produced by mere chance or incapable of being traced to any cause. It therefore affords no protection where the fire is caused by negligence or is due to a nuisance or arises from a non-natural user of land. Nor will the defendant escape liability if there is negligence in permitting an accidental fire to spread. In *Musgrove v. Pandelis* (C.A., 1919) the defendant was held liable when a fire started in the carburettor of his car in a garage without fault on anyone's part and his chauffeur negligently failed to extinguish it. It was also held that the 1774 Act was no defence to an action brought under *Rylands v. Fletcher*. However, if a domestic fire, intentionally lit, spreads without negligence the defendant is not liable (*Sochaki v. Sas* (H.C., 1947)). The Act also provided a defence in *Collingwood v. Home and Colonial Stores Ltd.* (C.A., 1936) where a fire broke out on the defendants' premises due to faulty electrical wiring but without negligence. In neither of these last two cases could *Rylands v. Fletcher* be invoked because there was no non-natural user of land.

---

13. LIABILITY FOR ANIMALS

COMMON LAW

A person may incur liability for damage caused by his animals in accordance with ordinary tort principles. Thus the crowing of cockerels may be actionable in nuisance (*Leeman v. Montagu* (H.C., 1936)), fox hunters may be liable in trespass if they cause their hounds to enter prohibited land (*League Against Cruel Sports Ltd v. Scott* (H.C., 1985)), and there have been numerous cases in which a person has been held liable in negligence because he owes the ordinary duty to take care that his animal is not put to such a use as is likely to injure his neighbour (Lord Atkin in *Fardon v. Harcourt-Rivington* (H.L., 1932)). A modern instance is *Draper v. Hodder* (C.A., 1972) where the defendant, whose terriers savaged the infant plaintiff, was held liable for failing to confine them. A defendant is generally not liable if animals naturally upon his land escape and do damage to his neighbour unless he was at fault in permitting their accumulation. Since the decision in *Goldman v. Hargrave* (P.C., 1967), however, he may be liable if, with knowledge of a potential threat (albeit not of his making), he fails to take reasonable steps to avert it.

Apart from the above, special rules relating to animals were developed at common law and these were modified by the Animals Act 1971. It should be noted that the Act, with which the remainder of this chapter is concerned, does not affect the availability of common law actions.

STRICT LIABILITY FOR DANGEROUS ANIMALS

The keeper of an animal was strictly liable at common law for damage done by the animal if either it belonged to a dangerous species or it did not so belong but he knew of its vicious characteristics. The 1971 Act preserves the distinction between dangerous and non-dangerous species.

Animals belonging to a dangerous species

By section 2(1) of the Act the keeper of an animal belonging to a dangerous species is liable for any damage caused by it. A dangerous species (which, by section 11, includes sub-species and variety) is one which is not commonly domesticated in the British Islands and whose fully-grown animals normally have such characteristics that they are likely, unless restrained, to cause severe damage or that any damage they may cause is likely to be severe (section 6(2)). With regard to the first part of this definition, the fact that an animal may be commonly domesticated in some other part of the world where it is indigenous, such as a camel, does not affect its classification as a dangerous species (*Tutin v. Chipperfield Promotions Ltd.* (H.C., 1980)). Furthermore, once a species has been so classified, the law takes no account of the fact that an individual animal within that species may in truth be harmless, so that the trained circus elephant is treated no differently to the wild elephant in the bush (*Behrens v. Bertram Mills Circus* (H.C., 1957)).

As far as the latter part of the definition is concerned, the species envisaged fall into two categories. First, there are those animals which are by natural disposition ferocious and, secondly, those which although normally peaceful have a potential for causing severe damage. There is no definition of "severe" and, by section 11, "damage" includes the death of, or injury to, any person (including any disease and any impairment of physical or mental condition). Since this is not an exhaustive definition the generally accepted view is that "damage" should be given its normal meaning which is wide enough to include damage to property.

Strict liability is thus imposed by section 2(1) but there is no indication in the Act as to what the test for remoteness should be. It has been suggested that, as long as a causal link is established between the animal and the damage, there is no need for the damage to be of a kind normally associated with the animal's characteristics. Support for this view is to be found in *Tutin v. Chipperfield Promotions Ltd.* (H.C., 1980) where the defendant was held liable for injuries suffered as a result of a fall from a swaying camel. It would therefore seem that the test is one of direct consequence rather than reasonable foresight.

Animals not belonging to a dangerous species

Strict liability is imposed by section 2(2) for harm done by animals not belonging to a dangerous species. Any animal not coming

within the definition of dangerous species in section 6(2) falls into
this category. The keeper is liable for damage caused by such an
animal if:

  (a) the damage is of a kind which the animal, unless restrained,
      was likely to cause or which, if caused by the animal, was
      likely to be severe; and

  (b) the likelihood of the damage or of its being severe was due
      to characteristics of the animal which are not normally found
      in animals of the same species, or are not normally so found
      except at particular times or in particular circumstances;
      and

  (c) those characteristics were known to the keeper or to any
      person in charge of the animal at the time as the keeper's
      servant or, where that keeper is the head of a household,
      were known to another keeper who is a member of that
      household and under the age of 16.

The operation of this section may be illustrated in the context of
Curtis v. Betts (C.A., 1990), where the plaintiff was attacked and
bitten by the defendant's bull mastiff (which was generally docile
and indolent) as it was being transferred into the rear of the family
car. With respect to paragraph (a) it was found that although the
damage in question was not of a kind which this dog, unless
restrained, was likely to cause, a bite from a bull mastiff was likely
to be severe, thus satisfying the second limb of the paragraph. In
relation to paragraph (b) it was found that the dog, in common
with its breed generally, was territorially defensive, and that the
likelihood of damage being severe was thus due to characteristics
which would not normally be found in bull mastiffs except in particular circumstances (*i.e.* when defending what they regarded as
their territory). The second limb of paragraph (b) was therefore
satisfied and, since on the evidence the defendant knew of his dog's
characteristics, he was liable under the Act even though not negligent. The earlier case of *Cummings v. Granger* (C.A., 1977) had
similarly held that injuries suffered by a person who entered the
domain of an Alsatian kept to guard premises fell within the second
limb of paragraph (b).

  In *Smith v. Ainger* (C.A., 1990) the keeper of a dog with a known
propensity to attack other dogs was held liable to a plaintiff who
was knocked over and injured by the dog in the course of its attack
upon the plaintiff's dog. In reaching this conclusion it was said that
the word "likely" in paragraph (a) did not mean "more probable
than not" but simply that there was a "material risk" that it would
happen. Since there was a material risk that the owner of a dog

being attacked would intervene to protect it, it followed that personal injury was likely to be caused within the meaning of the first limb of paragraph (a), and it was "unrealistic to distinguish between a bite and a buffet."

It is clear that the abnormal characteristics referred to in paragraph (b) do not mean that the animal must have a propensity to attack; nor need it escape from control (*Wallace v. Newton* (H.C., 1982)). The statutory provision also requires a comparison between the characteristics of the animal in question and those of animals of the same species (which includes sub-species and variety). Thus, in considering the characteristics of an Alsatian dog the relevant comparison is with other Alsatians, not dogs generally (*Hunt v. Wallis* (H.C., 1991)).

For the purposes of paragraph (c) the keeper must have actual, not merely constructive, knowledge of his animal's characteristics. Knowledge is however imputed to him where he is the head of a household and another keeper under the age of 16, being a member of that household, knew of those characteristics, or where a person in charge of the animal as the keeper's servant knew of them.

The keeper

Liability under section 2 is imposed upon the keeper who, by section 6(3), is the person who owns the animal or has it in his possession, or is the head of a household of which a member under the age of 16 owns it or has it in his possession. If a person ceases to own or have possession of the animal he will remain the keeper until such time as another person becomes the keeper. Thus, those who abandon unwanted pets do not thereby divest themselves of responsibility. A person who takes possession of an animal to prevent it from causing damage or to return it to its owner does not, merely by so doing, become a keeper.

Defences to liability under section 2

Apart from contributory negligence, which is preserved by section 10, section 5 of the Act contains a number of defences. Thus, there is no liability if the damage is wholly due to the plaintiff's fault (s.5(1)) or he voluntarily assumes the risk thereof (s.5(2)). The first of these defences will apply where, for example, the plaintiff deliberately provokes or teases the animal, or if he goes too close to its cage knowing that it is dangerous (*Marlor v. Ball* (C.A., 1900)). As far as the second is concerned, it should be noted that the Unfair Contract Terms Act 1977 does not apply to strict liability under the Animals Act so that a suitably worded notice may be sufficient to exclude liability. An important limitation upon the defence is that, by section 6(5), a keeper's servant is not to be treated as voluntarily accepting risks incidental to his employment. Section 5(3) applies to trespassers and provides that the keeper is not liable for damage done by an animal to persons trespassing upon the premises if either the animal was not kept there to protect persons or property or, if it was kept for that purpose, it was not unreasonable to do so. This does not affect the liability which a person may incur as an occupier under the Occupiers' Liability Act 1984 (see Chap. 8). Further, the Guard Dogs Act 1975 makes it a criminal offence to keep a guard dog on business premises (but not on agricultural land or land surrounding a private dwelling) unless either it is secured or under the control of a handler. In *Cummings v. Granger* (C.A., 1977) Lord Denning said that a keeper who contravenes the 1975 Act is therefore unlikely to be able to claim the protection of section 5(3) since it is doubtful whether he could then be said to be acting reasonably. In that case the plaintiff had entered the defendant's scrap-yard as a trespasser knowing that an Alsatian roamed the premises as a guard dog. It was held that, although the damage was not wholly due to the plaintiff's fault, she had nevertheless voluntarily assumed the risk and was also defeated by the defence in section 5(3) (the cause of action arose before the passing of the Guard Dog Act, so there was no question of the defendant's having committed an offence). No mention is made in the Act of act of a stranger or act of God, so that these are not available defences.

DOGS ATTACKING LIVESTOCK

Section 3 of the Animals Act imposes strict liability upon the keeper of a dog which causes damage by killing or injuring livestock. As well as the more common types of farm animal, "livestock" includes the domestic varieties of geese, ducks, guinea-fowl, pigeons, peacocks and quails, deer not in the wild state, and pheasants, partridges and grouse in captivity. As well as the defences in sections 10 and 5(1), it is a defence under section 5(4) that the livestock was killed or injured on land on to which it had strayed and the dog belonged to the occupier or its presence was authorised by him.

There is a defence in section 9 of the Act to an action for killing or injuring a dog. The defendant must prove that he acted for the protection of livestock and was entitled to do so, and that within 48 hours he notified the police. A person is entitled to act for their

protection if either the livestock or the land on which it is belongs
to him, or if he is acting under the express or implied authority of
such a person. He acts for their protection only if either of the
following conditions (satisfied by reasonable belief on his part
(s.9(4)) applies:

(a) the dog is worrying or is about to worry the livestock and
there are no other reasonable means of ending or preventing
the worrying; or

(b) the dog has been worrying livestock, has not left the vicinity,
is not under anyone's control, and there are no practicable
means of ascertaining to whom it belongs.

For the purpose of this section, the Act provides that livestock
belongs to a person who owns or has it in his possession and land
belongs to the occupier thereof (s.9(5)).

The defence in section 9 applies only to the protection of livestock from marauding dogs, so that if damage is caused to property
by other animals (for example homing pigeons eating crops as in
Hamps v. Darby (C.A., 1948)), or if for some reason the statutory
provisions are not satisfied, the defendant may fall back on the
common law as laid down in *Cresswell v. Sirl* (C.A., 1948). This
entitles the defendant to take punitive action if the animal is actually attacking his property or there is imminent danger that it will
renew an attack already made, and it is reasonable in the circumstances for the protection of that property to kill it.

STRAYING LIVESTOCK

Livestock straying on to another's land

By section 4(1) of the Act where livestock belonging to any person
strays on to land owned or occupied by another and causes damage
to the land or property in the ownership or possession of the other
person, the person to whom the livestock belongs is liable for the
damage. He is also liable for reasonable expenses incurred by the
other person in keeping the livestock while it cannot be restored
to the person to whom it belongs or while it is detained in pursu-
ance of section 7 (see below), or in ascertaining to whom it belongs.
The definition of livestock in section 11 is slightly narrower than
for the purposes of section 3 and 9 since it does not include captive
pheasants, partridges or grouse. Livestock belongs to the possessor
thereof, so that the owner out of possession, such as a finance company which has bailed the beasts under a hire-purchase agreement,
is not liable. There is no liability under this section for personal
injuries or third party property damage, which means that if such

damage is caused the action must be brought either in negligence or, if appropriate, under section 2(2) of the Act.

Defences

The defences laid down in sections 10 and 5(1) apply but, so far as the latter is concerned, section 5(6) provides that damage is not to be treated as due to the fault of the person suffering it by reason only that he could have prevented it by fencing. If, however, any person having an interest in the land is in breach of a duty to fence the defendant is not liable if the livestock would not have strayed but for that breach. It is plain from the statutory wording that the duty, if such there be, need not be owed by the plaintiff, nor need it be owed to the defendant. A final common law defence is preserved by section 5(5), which states that there is no liability for damage done by livestock which strays from the highway so long as its presence on the highway was lawful. This is not to say that a defendant may not be liable for negligence in such circumstances (*Gayler and Pope Ltd v. B. Davies & Son Ltd.* (H.C., 1924)).

Detention and sale of straying livestock

An occupier on to whose land livestock has strayed has a right under, and subject to the conditions of, section 7 to detain, and ultimately to sell, the livestock to recover the cost of damage done to his property.

STRAYING ON THE HIGHWAY

The common law immunity in respect of damage caused by animals straying on to the highway from adjacent land is abolished by section 8(1) of the Animals Act with the result that liability is now determined in accordance with ordinary negligence principles. A landowner is not necessarily obliged to fence his land, and if he does not, important factors in deciding whether he has been negligent are the prevailing traffic conditions, whether any warning has been given, and what users of the highway ought reasonably to expect. In particular, by section 8(2), if he has a right to place his animals on unfenced land he will not be in breach of a duty of care merely by placing them there, so long as the land is in an area where fencing is not customary or is common land or is a town or village green.

14. VICARIOUS LIABILITY

The general rule is that one who expressly authorises or ratifies a tort is personally liable, but there are circumstances in which a person is liable for the torts of another even in the absence of such authorisation or ratification. The liability which thus arises is known as vicarious liability and the most common example of it is the liability of a master for the torts of his servants committed in the course of their employment.

MASTER AND SERVANT

It is not necessary, for the purposes of the doctrine, that the master be in breach of any duty owed to the injured party (who may himself be either a fellow-servant or a stranger). What is required is that the wrongdoer be a servant and the wrong done in connection with what he is employed to do. The modern justification for the doctrine is that the master is better able to pay because he will insure against such liability, the cost of which is reflected in the price charged for his goods and services. It is also said to act as an inducement to the employer to promote high standards of safety within his organisation.

The meaning of servant

A servant is employed under a contract of service, an independent contractor under a contract for services, but this does not explain the essential distinction between the two types of contract. No single test has yet been devised which is capable of application in all cases, and even the express declaration of the parties as to the nature of their contract is simply one factor to be taken into account (*Ferguson v. John Dawson & Partners (Contractors) Ltd.* (C.A., 1976)). If the employer controls not only the type of work to be done but also the manner in which it is to be done, that points to a contract of service; but this so-called "control" test has, especially where the task to be performed requires a high degree of skill or expertise, lost much of its use, for the servant will in practice frequently be left to decide for himself how best to carry out the job. In *Stevenson, Jordan and Harrison Ltd. v. Macdonald and Evans* (C.A., 1952) Denning L.J. suggested that, under a contract of service, the employee's work is done as an integral part of the business, whereas under a contract for services his work is not integrated into the business but is merely accessory to it. More recently, in *Ready Mixed*

Concrete (South East) Ltd. v. Minister of Pensions and National Insurance
(H.C., 1968) it was held that three conditions must be fulfilled for
a contract of service to exist. First, the servant agrees, in consideration of a wage or other remuneration, to provide his own work and
skill in the performance of some service for his master; secondly,
he agrees to be subject to the other's control to such degree as to
make that other the master; thirdly, the other provisions of the
contract are consistent with its being a contract of service. A different approach was adopted in *Market Investigations Ltd. v. Minister of
Social Security* (H.C., 1969) where it was suggested that the basic
test is whether the worker is performing the service as a person in
business on his own account. In answering this question it is relevant to consider whether the person uses his own premises and
equipment, whether he hires his own helpers, the degree of financial risk he takes and the degree of responsibility, if any, which he
has for investment and management. Although this approach has
been followed in later cases, judicial warnings have been given that
the test is not of itself to be regarded as conclusive of the question.
All that can be said is that there is no exhaustive category of matters relevant in deciding the issue, and what is regarded as the
crucial factor in one case may well be outweighed by different considerations in another.

Lending a servant

A particular problem is that of lending a servant, for the difficulty
then arises as to who is the master for the purposes of vicarious
liability. In *Mersey Docks and Harbour Board v. Coggins and Griffith
(Liverpool) Ltd.* (H.L., 1947) the Board hired a crane driver, together
with his crane, to X, under a contract which provided that the
driver was to be the servant of X. In the course of working the
crane the driver negligently injured a third party. Although X had,
at the time, the immediate direction and control of what was to be
done, they had no power to direct how the crane should be worked.
Furthermore, the driver continued to be paid by the Board, which
alone had the right to dismiss him. It was held that, notwithstanding the terms of the hire contract, the Board had failed to discharge
the heavy burden of proof to shift responsibility for the driver's
negligence onto X. This case establishes no universal test but Lord
Porter said that factors for consideration are who is paymaster,
who can dismiss, how long the alternative service lasts and what
machinery is employed. The degree of control exercised by the
respective employers is clearly important, and it would seem that

the right to control is more readily transferred in the case of an unskilled servant.

The course of employment

For the master to be liable the wrong must be committed in the course of the servant's employment. This will be the case where what the servant does is authorised by the master, or is an unauthorised way of doing that which he is employed to do. Whether or not the act is done in the course of employment is a question of fact, and the modern trend has been to adopt a liberal approach. Thus, a tanker driver who, whilst delivering petrol, lit a cigarette and carelessly discarded a match causing a fire, was held to be acting within the course of his employment. It was said that the act of lighting the cigarette, whilst not in itself connected with his job, could not be looked at in isolation from the surrounding circumstances (*Century Insurance Co. Ltd. v. Northern Ireland Road Transport Board* (H.L., 1942)).

If, on the other hand, the servant's act is wholly unconnected to the job for which he is employed, he is said to be "on a frolic of his own" and the master is not liable. In *Beard v. London General Omnibus Co.* (C.A., 1900) the employer of a bus conductor who, in the absence of the driver, negligently drove the bus himself was held not liable. This may be contrasted with *Kay v. I.T.W. Ltd* (C.A., 1968) where the servant attempted to move a lorry belonging to another firm because it was blocking the entrance to his employer's warehouse to which he had been instructed to return a fork-lift truck. It was held that, since the attempted removal of the obstruction was done in order that the servant could complete his own task, the employer was vicariously liable. On the other hand, it was held in *General Engineering Services Ltd. v. Kingston and St. Andrew Corp.* (P.C., 1988) that firemen operating a "go-slow" policy who took five times as long as they normally would have done to drive to the scene of a fire (with the result that the plaintiff's premises were destroyed) were not within the course of employment. The courts have been faced with similar problems where the servant's act has been expressly prohibited. In principle, if the prohibition amounts to a restriction on the class of acts which the servant is employed to do, the master is not liable; but he is liable if the prohibition relates merely to a mode of performing the employment. So a servant who, contrary to written instructions, raced his employer's bus with that of a rival company was held to be within the course of his employment (*Limpus v. London General Omnibus Co.*,

(H.C., 1862)). A number of cases have dealt with the problem of the giving of lifts to unauthorised passengers. It was held in *Twine v. Bean's Express Ltd.* (C.A., 1946) that such an act was outside the course of employment, though the view was expressed that, in so far as injury to persons other than the passenger was concerned, the driver would be within the course of his employment. Where a driver's foreman consented to the passenger's presence in the vehicle, however, the master was held liable because the foreman, of whose lack of actual authority the passenger was unaware, was nonetheless acting within the scope of his apparent authority (*Young v. Edward Box & Co. Ltd.* (C.A., 1951)). The decision in *Twine*'s case is not easy to reconcile with *Rose v. Plenty* (C.A., 1976) where a milkman, in allowing a young boy onto his float to help him with his milk round in contravention of his employer's instructions, was held to be within the course of his employment when the boy fell off and was injured. The majority of the court distinguished the earlier case on the ground that the engagement of the boy was done in furtherance of the master's business.

There are cases where the servant's act, although not part of his regular employment as such, is necessarily incidental to it. In *Staton v. National Coal Board* (H.C., 1957), for example, a servant cycling to the pay office on his employer's land to collect his pay after work had finished was held to be within the course of his employment. But whilst employment may start as soon as the servant enters his employer's premises, those travelling to or from work are not usually considered to be in the course of employment, unless, of course, they are travelling specifically on the master's business or on some errand which is incidental to it. Thus, a driver who deviates from his route for the purpose of getting a meal may still be within the course of employment (*Harvey v. R. G. O'Dell Ltd.* (H.C., 1958); *cf. Hilton v. Thomas Burton (Rhodes) Ltd.* (H.C., 1961)). In *Smith v. Stages* (H.L., 1989) a worker travelling between home and a temporary workplace, and who was paid wages during that time, was held to be within the course of employment, notwithstanding that he might have a discretion as to the mode and time of travel.

A servant who uses force in the mistaken but honest belief that he is protecting his master's property does an act incidental to his employment rendering the master liable (*Poland v. John Parr & Sons* (C.A., 1927)). Clearly, though, punishment administered during the course of a private altercation which ensues after the need to protect the master's property no longer exists is not within the course of employment (*Warren v. Henlys Ltd.* (H.C., 1948)).

The final question to be considered is the extent of a master's liability for the servant who acts dishonestly for his own benefit. In *Morris v. C. W. Martin & Sons Ltd.* (C.A., 1966) the defendants' employee stole a coat entrusted to him for cleaning. Whether, as was suggested, the defendants were in breach of their primary duty as bailees, they could equally have been regarded as vicariously liable for their servant's wrongful mode of performing that which he was employed to do, namely to keep the coat safe for its owner. This case has since been approved by the Privy Council. A different problem emerges where the servant abuses his position for fraudulent purposes. In this case, if a master makes it appear to third parties that the servant has authority to do acts of the type in question, he may be estopped from denying that the servant had any authority in fact. It is not enough that the servant's employment provides an opportunity for the commission of the wrong. The essential feature is that it is the position in which the employer places his servant that enables him to perpetrate the fraud whilst acting within the scope of the authority that he appears to have. Thus, in *Lloyd v. Grace Smith & Co.* (H.L., 1912) solicitors were held liable for the fraud of their managing clerk in inducing the plaintiff to execute documents which he falsely stated were necessary to effect a sale of her cottages, but which amounted to a conveyance of the property to himself. In fraud cases, therefore, the parameters of the course of employment are set by the scope of authority so that, in *Armagas Ltd. v. Mundogas S.A.* (C.A., 1985) the plaintiff's contention that a servant could be acting beyond the scope of his authority but within the course of his employment was rejected. Similarly, if the plaintiff is unaware that the fraudulent servant is the defendant's employee he cannot claim to have relied upon the servant's apparent authority and the defendant will not be liable unless, of course, the servant was within the scope of his actual authority (*Kooragang Investments Pty. Ltd v. Richardson & Wrench Ltd* (P.C., 1982)).

Joint liability

Where a servant commits a tort in the course of his employment both he and his master are liable as joint tortfeasors. This means that if the master satisfies the judgment he may be able to claim contribution from his servant under the Civil Liability (Contribution) Act 1978. Additionally he may (at least in theory) be able to recover from his servant under the principle in *Lister v. Romford Ice and Cold Storage Co. Ltd* (H.L., 1957) where damages equivalent to an indemnity were awarded to a master, who, having met the plaintiff's claim, sued his negligent employee for breach of an implied term of his employment contract that he would exercise reasonable care. In practice, however, the *Lister* principle is virtually defunct in view of an undertaking by employers' liability insurers that they would not seek to recover from an individual employee except where there was evidence of collusion or wilful misconduct.

INDEPENDENT CONTRACTORS

In general, an employer is not vicariously liable for the negligence of an independent contractor in carrying out his work. He is of course liable if he authorises or ratifies the tort, as he is if he is personally negligent, for example by selecting an incompetent contractor or failing to give proper instructions or supervision. In addition, he may be under a non-delegable duty of care which cannot be discharged merely by entrusting performance to a contractor. It is worth noting that liability in all of these instances is not vicarious but arises as a result of a breach of a primary duty owed by the employer to the plaintiff. The remainder of this section deals with the employer's so-called non-delegable duties.

Common law

1. Withdrawal of support from neighbouring land

Where one of two adjoining landowners is entitled to support from the other and that other, either himself or through his contractor, undermines that support causing damage to his neighbour's land or building, he is liable (*Bower v. Peate* (H.C., 1876)). This principle was extended in *Alcock v. Wraith* (C.A., 1991) to impose a duty on the owner of a house who, in order to repair his roof, necessarily had to interfere with the integrity of his neighbour's roof.

2. Operations on the highway

Where a contractor is employed to do work on or adjoining the highway which creates a danger to users of the highway, the employer remains liable. So, in *Tarry v. Ashton* (H.C., 1876), where a contractor negligently fitted a lamp to the side of a house with the result that it fell and injured a passer-by, the employer was held liable. Although this principle applies to dangers created in any place along which the public may lawfully pass, no liability attaches to a person using the highway merely for the purposes of lawful passage. Thus, if a motor vehicle is negligently repaired by a contractor, the owner is not liable for an accident caused by the unroadworthy state of the vehicle. (*Phillips v. Britannia Hygienic Laundry Co. Ltd* (H.C, 1923)). Nor is their liability in respect of work carried out near the highway. In *Salsbury v. Woodland* (C.A., 1970), the employer was held not liable when his contractor negligently cut down a tree in his front garden and, in so doing, fouled some telephone wires which collapsed onto the highway and caused an accident.

3. Master's duty to servant
The non-delegable nature of this common law duty is deal with in Chapter 7.

4. Extra-hazardous activities
Where the contractor's work, by its very nature, involves a special danger to others, it seems that the employer will be liable for the contractor's default. In *Honeywill and Stein Ltd. v. Larkin Bros. Ltd* (C.A., 1934) the plaintiffs were held liable where the defendants, whom they had employed to take photographs inside a theatre, negligently caused a fire in their use of magnesium flash powder. This principle probably applies only to acts involving the use of things regarded in law as "dangerous in themselves," of which fire and explosives are obvious examples. Since there is nothing inherently dangerous in the operation of felling a tree, *Salsbury v. Woodland* (C.A., 1970) was held not to come within this head of liability.

5. Nuisance, Rylands v. Fletcher and fire
The extent of an employer's liability in these instances is dealt with in Chapters 11 and 12.

6. Other cases
There seems to be no general principle which can be extracted from the examples discussed, and the courts may come to recognise new types of case giving rise to a non-delegable duty. A recent illustration is *Rogers v. Night Riders* (C.A., 1983) in which the plaintiff was injured when the door of a mini-cab flew open. Although the vehicle was owned and maintained by the driver, an independent contractor, the mini-cab firm was nevertheless held to be in breach of a primary duty owed to the plaintiff.

Statutory duties
Where a statute imposes an obligation upon a person to do a particular thing, he cannot escape liability by delegation to an independent contractor. If the statute empowers a person to do some-

thing which would otherwise be unlawful, that person will generally be liable of the negligence of his contractor (*Hardaker v. Idle D.C.* (C.A., 1896)). The precise nature of the duty depends, for however, upon the construction of the Act.

Casual or collateral negligence

It is the nature of the work, and not merely the performance of it, which may cast upon the employer a non-delegable duty. He is therefore not liable for the casual or collateral negligence of his independent contractor because that does not involve him in any breach of duty. Collateral negligence is negligence purely incidental to the particular act the contractor was employed to do. Thus, in *Padbury v. Holliday and Greenwood Ltd.* (C.A., 1912) the defendants were not liable when their sub-contractor, in fixing a casement, negligently left a tool on the window sill which the wind blew onto a passer-by below. By contrast, in *Holliday v. National Telephone Co.* (C.A., 1899) the defendants employed a plumber to carry out work on the highway. The plumber negligently dipped his blowlamp into molten solder and the plaintiff was injured in the ensuing explosion. Reversing the decision of the Divisional Court, the Court of Appeal held the employer liable, though the distinction between this and the *Padbury* case is not easy to see.

VEHICLE OWNERS

A vehicle owner who allows another to drive it in his presence makes such a person his agent and is liable for his negligent driving. So too, if a person has authority to drive on behalf of, or for the purposes of, the owner, the latter is vicariously liable for his negligence even though not himself present in the vehicle (*Ormrod v. Crosville Motor Services Ltd.* (C.A., 1953)). The leading case of *Launchbury v. Morgans* (H.L., 1973) establishes that the owner is not liable simply for permitting another to use the vehicle for his own purposes. It must be shown that the driver was using it for the owner's purposes under delegation of some task or duty, and the mere fact that the owner has an interest in the safety of the vehicle's occupants is not sufficient. Nor, according to *Norwood v. Navan* (C.A., 1981), is a wife who uses her husband's car to go on a shopping expedition acting for his purposes under delegation of a task or duty so as to make him vicariously liable.

15. SAMPLE EXAMINATION QUESTIONS AND ANSWER PLANS

QUESTION 1

Frost, a school teacher, takes a party of children to Marshmoor one Saturday in February for a day's nature ramble. Marshmoor is locally known for the sudden mists which from time to time descend over the region, though Frost is unaware of this.

Early in the afternoon a thick mist envelops the area and the temperature drops rapidly. Frost has forgotten to bring with him his map and compass, and the group becomes hopelessly lost. After rambling aimlessly for some considerable time the party takes shelter in a derelict barn to wait for the mist to clear.

Meanwhile, when Frost fails to return home at the expected time, his wife contacts the police and a local search party is mounted. Jones, a member of the rescue party, misses his footing on a steep bank and falls and breaks his leg. When Frost and the children are eventually found later that night they are all taken to hospital suffering from the effects of exposure and one of them, Harry, is found to have frostbite. The children's parents are informed of what has happened and Harry's mother, Iris, watches a television news bulletin which shows the children being taken from the ambulance into hospital. Iris, who is of a nervous disposition, is now suffering from shock.

Advise the injured parties of their rights of action, if any, in tort.

ANSWER PLAN

Harry and his schoolfriends, Jones and Iris may bring an action against Frost in the tort of negligence. Briefly define negligence as a tort.

1. Harry and friends v. Frost

(a) Frost clearly owes a duty to the children whom he ought reasonably to have foreseen would be likely to suffer personal injury as a result of his acts or omissions (Lord Atkin in *Donoghue v. Stevenson* – the neighbour principle). The other formal requirements for the existence of a duty are clearly satisfied in this case.

(b) Explain the legal standard of care and the application of that standard to the particular facts, having regard to the degree of risk and the ease with which Frost could have taken pre-

cautions to guard against it (*e.g.* check on the terrain and the weather (note the time of year), take map and compass, warn about suitable clothing, etc.). It seems that Frost is in breach of duty.
  (c) Applying the "but for" test Frost's breach causes the damage in question, which is foreseeable in kind and therefore not too remote (see *The Wagon Mound*). The fact that the injury to Harry may be greater in extent than could have been foreseen is irrelevant (*Hughes v. Lord Advocate*; *Bradford v. Robinson Rentals*).
  (d) Frost would therefore be liable and there appear to be no defences on the facts.

2. Jones v. Frost

  (a) Where F., by his negligence, imperils the safety of others, such that it is reasonably foreseeable that a person such as Jones will attempt a rescue, F. owes a duty directly to J. and will be liable for any injury foreseeably sustained by him in the course of the rescue attempt (*Haynes v. Harwood*).
  (b) The volenti defence will not apply, nor will J.'s conduct break the chain of causation (*Haynes v. Harwood*). Contributory negligence may be a partial defence if J. shows a wanton disregard for his own safety (*Baker v. Hopkins*), but no evidence of this appears from the facts.

3. Iris v. Frost

The shock must manifest itself in some recognisable psychiatric illness. For a duty to be owed Iris must, as a passive witness to the events, prove that her relationship to the primary victim was one of close love and affection, that she was spatially and temporally proximate to the scene of the accident, and that the shock was produced through sight or hearing of the event. Although there may possibly be liability for shock induced by contemporaneous broadcast of the event, the plaintiff must in all cases show that a person of reasonable fortitude might foreseeably have suffered shock. Applying these criteria to the facts Iris's claim is very unlikely to succeed; see *Alcock v. Chief Constable of South Yorkshire*.

4. All Parties v. Frost's Employer

Consider the possible vicarious liability of F.'s employer with particular regard to whether he was acting within the course of his employment.

QUESTION 2

Fisher and Company import a quantity of Canadian salmon into this country and sell it to Batter Ltd, who use it to make salmon paté. Those parts of the fish which are not used are supplied by Batter Ltd to Rex plc, who use it in the manufacture of dog food.

Amy buys several jars of the salmon paté, together with a tin of the dog food from Pricebuster plc, a supermarket chain. She uses the paté to make sandwiches for sale at the local church fair. Laura buys one of the sandwiches for her husband Dean, who becomes violently ill after eating it. Amy's dog suffers a similar fate after eating the dog food, in consequence of which Amy incurs expensive veterinary surgeon's costs.

It is subsequently discovered that the fish farming process in Canada involves treating the water with a chemical compound designed to kill lice, which are otherwise prone to infest the salmon. A recent article in a national food science journal criticised the use of the chemical on the ground that there was evidence that it could produce a severe allergic reaction in certain people.

Advise Amy and Dean, ignoring any possible liability of the Canadian fish farmer.

ANSWER PLAN

1. Amy's claim under the Consumer Protection Act 1987

(a) Amy must prove that she suffered damage (*i.e.* injury to her dog, the value of which may be measured by reference to the vet's costs) caused wholly or partly by a defect in a product.

(b) Consider the potential range of defendants *viz.* Fisher and Co. as importer, Batter Ltd and Rex plc as producers and Pricebuster plc as possible own brander; see s.2(2) and s.1(2).

(c) Note, however, that no person is liable for defects in agricultural produce (which includes fisheries) if at the time he supplied it to another it had not undergone an industrial process. Thus, Fisher and Co. will not be liable unless something done to or with the fish in Canada (*e.g.* treating the water) could be regarded as such a process (see s.2(4)). Note, however, that once the product has been subjected to an industrial process it is irrelevant for the purposes of establishing liability that the defect had nothing to do with that process.

(d) Consider whether the product is defective within the meaning of s.3. If it is the defendant is strictly liable for the damage subject to any defence. However, in respect of property damage there is no liability unless its value exceeds £275, in which case the plaintiff must sue in negligence.

(e) Consider possible defences, in particular the so-called "development risks" defence in s.4(1)(e). Contrast with Article 7 of the Directive and note that s.1(1) of the Act states that the purpose of Part I is to give effect to the Directive and should be construed accordingly.

2. Amy's claim in negligence

(a) A duty is owed by the manufacturer of a product to the ultimate consumer in accordance with the narrow ratio in *Donoghue v. Stevenson*.

(b) Despite the judicial extension of the term "manufacturer" to include, for example, a mere supplier (*Fisher v. Harrods*; *Andrews v. Hopkinson*), there may be some difficulty in establishing negligence especially since the apparent defect existed before the product was imported into the country. Even if the defendant knew that the chemical was used for treating the fish, it would further have to be shown that he knew or ought to have known of, or ought to have taken steps to find out about, possible harmful side effects, and that he failed to give adequate warning. If this could be proved, the ordinary principles of causation and remoteness apply.

3. Dean's claim under the Act

The same considerations relevant to Amy's claim generally apply to Dean except that he suffers only personal injury so the £275 limit does not apply, and Rex plc are not potential defendants though Amy (as a supplier) may be. However, if she complied with a request to identify the person who supplied the salmon to her, her liability would cease. In any event there would seem to be a clear defence under s.4(1)(c).

4. Dean's claim in negligence

The same considerations as for Amy's claim would apply. Note that there is no evidence whatsoever that Amy was herself negligent.

QUESTION 3

Lord Summerset owns a private estate where members of the public are permitted to fish upon payment for a licence. Perkins is employed as a warden to deter poachers and patrols the estate with Tarzan, a large Alsatian dog.

Black and White, who both have a licence, enter the estate to go fishing. While crossing a wooden bridge over the river Black's foot goes through a rotten plank of wood and his leg is badly injured. Lord Summerset had recently had extensive repair work done on the bridge by Alpha Ltd, a firm of contractors.

White, who is fishing peacefully from the river bank, is approached by Perkins and Tarzan. White has a fear of dogs and starts to run away. Tarzan gives chase, as he has been trained to do, and White stumbles down the bank into the river, striking his head on a large rock.

Green, a boy of thirteen who does not have a licence, also enters the estate. As he is playing along the river bank he trips and falls, cutting himself severely on a broken glass bottle. Perkins had on a number of occasions told Lord Summerset about the rubbish left behind by visitors to the estate.

Discuss the rights and liabilities of the parties.

ANSWER PLAN

1. Black v. Lord Summerset

(a) Black may have an action against Lord S. for negligence. As a person who would have been an invitee or licensee at common law B. is a visitor under the Occupiers' Liability Act 1957 (s.1(2)), and Lord S. is an occupier because he has sufficient control over the premises to put him under a duty to those who come lawfully onto them (*Wheat v. Lacon*). Lord S. therefore owes to B. the common duty of care (s.2(1)), as defined in s.2(2) of the Act.

(b) In determining whether Lord S. is in breach of the duty ordinary negligence principles apply, but particular regard should be had to s.2(4)(b) concerning faulty repair work done by an independent contractor. This provides that Lord S. will have discharged the duty if he acted reasonably in entrusting the work to a contractor and took such steps (if any) as he reasonably ought to see that Alpha was competent and had done the work properly. It was no doubt reasonable to entrust work of the nature in question to a contractor, but there is no evidence as to whether Lord S. took any further steps. In the case of technical work he may be entitled to leave it to an apparently competent contractor (*Haseldine v. Daw*) unless it is of such a nature as to require supervision by another expert, as may be the case in a complex building project (*AMF International v. Magnet Bowling*). On the other hand, if a cursory check by Lord S. himself would have revealed the rotten plank he will remain liable. Whether or not Lord S. is liable, Alpha may be for breach of their common law duty of care. Note that the normal principles of causation and remoteness apply to an action for breach of duty under the 1957 Act. No defences are available on the facts.

2. White v. Lord S. and/or Perkins

(a) W. may have an action against Lord S. and/or P. under the Animals Act 1971 if either or both fall within the definition of "keeper" (see s.6(3)).

(b) Since the dog does not belong to a dangerous species (*Cummings v. Granger*) the provisions of s.2(2) must be considered and applied to the facts. Was the damage of a kind which Tarzan was likely to cause, or which, if caused, was likely to be severe (note that there is no direct infliction of damage by the dog)? See s.2(2)(a). If so, was this due to abnormal characteristics not normally found in other Alsatians (see *Hunt v. Wallis*), or not normally so found except at particular times or in particular circumstances (*e.g.* when acting as a patrol dog and seeing someone on its territory take flight)? See s.2(2)(b). These characteristics must be known to the keeper or, if P. was Lord S.'s employee, knowledge on P.'s part would be sufficient to hold Lord S. liable. See s.2(2)(c). Liability is strict subject to any defence.

(c) P. could be liable in accordance with ordinary negligence principles for failing to take reasonable care properly to control the dog and, if he is an employee, Lord S. could be vicariously liable.

(d) There may be a possible defence of contributory negligence, if, by running away from the dog, W. could be regarded as having failed to take reasonable care for his own safety but, given his fear of dogs, this is very unlikely. This defence is available both to a common law action and to an action under the 1971 Act. N.B. The provisions of the Law Reform (Contributory Negligence) Act 1945.

3. Green v. Lord S.

Since G. does not have a licence and enters the premises to play, he would appear to be a trespasser. As such Lord S. would owe a duty to him only if the three conditions in s.1(3) of the Occupiers' Liability Act 1984 were satisfied. Although Lord S. is aware of the "danger" from discarded rubbish he may not be aware of the specific danger of broken glass (see s.1(3)(a)). There is no evidence as to whether he knows or has reasonable grounds to believe that G. may come into the vicinity of the danger (see s.1(3)(b)), and the risk may not be sufficiently serious such that he ought reasonably to have guarded against it (see s.1(3)(c)). If a duty is owed to G. it is to take reasonable care to see that he is not injured by reason of the danger concerned, which is the ordinary duty in negligence generally.

QUESTION 4

Harvey goes out one evening with a group of friends to a public house to celebrate his forthcoming marriage to Melissa. Towards the end of the evening Greg, who was at one time engaged to Melissa, goes into the pub in a state of inebriation and sees Harvey. He lurches to the table where Harvey is sitting and says in a loud voice: "I hear you're getting married to that drunken slut. You ought to see a psychiatrist." Melissa was, until recently, a registered alcoholic but has since been cured of her problem.

Angered by these remarks Harvey rushes from his seat threatening to break Greg's neck. Greg staggers backwards and collides with Iris, a barmaid, who falls and breaks her arm. Lola, the publican, locks the door and refuses to let anyone leave the premises until the police arrive.

Advise the parties of their possible rights of action in tort.

ANSWER PLAN

1. Harvey v. Greg
H. may have an action against G. in defamation, more specifically slander.

    (a) H. must first prove that the statement is defamatory, so a definition is required. The judge must decide whether it is capable of being defamatory in law, and the jury whether it is in fact. If persons to whom the words were published would reasonably understand them as mere abuse they may not, as in this case, be defamatory. However, the statement would appear to be prima facie defamatory, and the question is one for the jury.

    (b) Distinction between libel and slander. Would the words in

this case be actionable *per se* or would H. have to prove special damage (see, *e.g.*, s.2 Defamation Act 1952)?

(c) H. must prove that the statement refers to him and was
published to a third party, which presents no problem here.

(d) Before considering defences the meaning properly to be
ascribed to the words should be ascertained, *e.g.* does the
suggestion that H. should "see a psychiatrist" impute some
sort of mental instability? If so, could it possibly be justified?
It seems clear from these facts that no defence would be
available.

2. Melissa v. Greg

M. could also sue for slander upon proof that the statement was
defamatory, that it referred to her and that it was published. See
Harry above.

(a) Would the words be actionable *per se*? What does the meaning of the word "slut" convey? N.B. Slander of Women Act
1891.

(b) Could the fact that M. was formerly a registered alcoholic
be relied upon by G. in a plea of justification? As with Harry
there appear to be no viable defences on the facts.

3. Greg v. Harvey

G. could bring an action against H. in trespass for assault.

(a) Define assault. Could H's threat to break G's neck in itself
amount to assault? See *Meade*'s case and *cf. R. v. Wilson*,
though note that in this case H. rushes from his seat.

(b) Consider whether any defence would be available to H. *e.g.*
contributory negligence, volenti non fit injuria (see *Murphy
v. Culhane*; *Barnes v. Nayer*).

4. Iris v. Harvey and Greg

It is unlikely that I could sue H. for assault and/or battery in the
absence of any act directed towards her, unless the doctrine of
transferred intent could apply in these circumstances. She might,
however, succeed in an action for negligence against both H. and
G. on the ground that the fracas created on a foreseeable risk of
injury to others on the premises.

5. Customers v. Lola

(a) Define false imprisonment and consider whether an action
would lie.

(b) Consider whether any defence would be available *e.g.* see *Albert v. Lavin*, though it is doubtful whether this would avail in respect of customers who were in no way involved in the argument.

INDEX

ABNORMAL SENSITIVITY,
  unreasonable interference and, 95
ABSOLUTE PRIVILEGE,
  defamation, defence to action for, 89
ACT OF GOD,
  strict liability, defence to claim for,
    109
ANIMALS, LIABILITY FOR,
  common law, 112
  dogs attacking livestock, 116–117
  highway, straying on, 118
  livestock,
    dogs attacking, 116–117
    highway, straying on, 118
    straying, 117–118
  strict liability for dangerous animals,
    belonging to dangerous species,
      113
    defences to liability, 115–116
    generally, 112–113
    keeper, 115
    not belonging to dangerous
      species, 113–115
ANNOYANCE,
  intentional, 96–97
  nuisance. See Nuisance
APOLOGY,
  defamation, defence to action for,
    91–92
APPORTIONMENT,
  contributory negligence, of, 47–48
ARREST,
  lawful, as defence to trespass to
    person, 10
  unlawful, as false imprisonment,
    4–5
ASSAULT,
  battery compared with, 3–4
  meaning, 3

BATTERY,
  assault compared with, 3–4
  examples, 2
  hostile, meaning, 1–2
  interference, nature of, 2–3
  meaning, 1
  physical force, application of, 1
BREACH OF DUTY,
  care, duty of. See CARE, DUTY OF
  statutory duty. See STATUTORY DUTY,
    BREACH OF

CAR PASSENGERS,
  contributory negligence, 47
  volenti non fit injuria, 50
CARE, DUTY OF,
  breach of duty,
    characteristics of defendant, 31–33
    evidence of negligence, 33–34
    reasonable man, 28–29
    risk, concept of, 29–31
  economic loss,
    negligent acts, 19–23
    negligent mis-statement, 14–15
  establishing duty,
    forseeability, 11–12
    generally, 10–11
    just and reasonable requirements,
      12
    present position, 13–14
    proximity, 11–12
    public policy, 12–13
  generally, 10
  Hedley Byrne,
    application of, 16–17
    contributory negligence, 17–18
    disclaimers, 17–18
    generally, 15
    subsequent developments, 15–16
    third party, reliance by, 18–19
  legal immunities, 27–28
  nervous shock, 23–25
  occupier's liability,
    children, relating to, 71
    damage, 73
    defences, 73
    generally, 70
    independent contractors, 72–73
    special skills, 71–72
    warnings, 72
  omissions, 25–27
  standard of care, causation and, 45
CAUSATION,
  contributory negligence, 45
  dangerous products, liability for,
    59–60
  factual, 35–37
  statutory duty, breach of, 79–80
CHARACTERISTICS OF DEFENDANT,
  children, 31–32
  generally, 31
  professionals, 32–33

CHILD,
  breach of duty of care, 31–32
  contributory negligence, 45–46
  occupier's liability, 71
COMMON LAW,
  animals, liability for, 112
  contributory negligence, 44
  dangerous products, liability for,
    causation, 59–60
    damage, 60–61
    generally, 58
    intermediate examination, 59–60
    manufacturer's duty, 58–59
    manufacturer, 59
    proof of negligence, 60–61
  employer's liability at. *See*
    EMPLOYER'S LIABILITY
  fire, escape of, 111
CONSENT,
  plaintiff, of, strict liability and, 110
  trespass to person, defence to, 8–9
CONTRACTORS. *See* INDEPENDENT
    CONTRACTORS
CONTRIBUTORY NEGLIGENCE
  apportionment, 47–48
  car passengers, 47
  causation, 45
  children, 45–46
  common law, 44
  defence of, 44–45
  generally, 44–45
  Hedley Byrne, application of, 17–18
  infirm person, 46
  old person, 46
  particular cases, 45–47
  rescuers, 46
  standard of care, 45
  statutory duty, breach of, 81
  trespass to person, defence to, 9
  workmen, 46–47

DAMAGE
  dangerous products, liability for,
    55–56, 60–61
  occupier's liability, 73
  private nuisance, 97
  remoteness of,
    competing tests, 37–38
    egg-shell skull rule, 39–40
    extent of damage, 39–40
    generally, 35
    manner of occurrence, 38
    strict liability and, 108
    type of damage, 38–39
  statutory duty, breach of, 79
  third party property, to, 19–20

DAMAGES,
  trespass, in, 7
DANGEROUS ANIMALS. *See* ANIMALS,
    LIABILITY FOR
DANGEROUS PRODUCTS,
  common law negligence,
    generally, 58
    intermediate examination and
      causation, 59–60
    manufacturer, meaning, 59
    manufacturer's duty, 58–59
    proof of negligence and damage,
      60–61
    ultimate consumer, 59
  liability for, 52–58
  strict liability under 1987 Act,
    damage, 55–56
    defect, meaning, 54–55
    defences, 56–57
    generally, 53
    miscellaneous, 57–58
    parties to action, 53–54
    product, meaning, 53–54
DEFAMATION,
  defences,
    absolute privilege, 89
    apology, 91–92
    fair comment, 88–89
    justification, 87
    qualified privilege, 90–91
    unintentional defamation, 86–87
  future reform, 92
  generally, 81–82
  libel and slander, 82–83
  proof required of plaintiff,
    publication, 85–86
    reference to plaintiff, 85
    statement must be defamatory,
      83–85
  unintentional, 86–87
DEFECT,
  meaning, 54–55
DEFECTIVE PROPERTY,
  acquisition of, 20–23
DEFENCES,
  dangerous products, liability for,
    56–57
  defamation, action for,
    absolute privilege, 89
    apology, 91–92
    fair comment, 88–89
    justification, 87
    qualified privilege, 90–91
    unintentional defamation, 86–87
  nuisance, action for,
    coming to nuisance, 101
    other defences, 101

DEFENCES—*cont.*
  prescription, 100
  statutory authority, 100–101
  occupier's liability, 73
  statutory duty, breach of,
    contributory negligence, 81
    delegation, 81
    volenti non fit injuria, 81
    straying livestock, 118
  strict liability,
    act of God, 109
    consent of plaintiff, 110
    dangerous animals, strict liability
      for, 115–116
    default of plaintiff, 110
    generally, 109
    statutory authority, 110
    stranger, act of, 109–110
  trespass to person, to,
    availability of, 8
    consent, 8–9
    contributory negligence, 9
    lawful arrest, 10
    necessity, 9
    self-defence, 9–10
DEFENDANT,
  characteristics of,
    children, 31–32
    generally, 31
    professionals, 32–33
  statutory duty, breach of, 78–79
DELEGATION,
  employer's liability, of, 65–66
  statutory duty, breach of, 81
DISCLAIMER,
  Hedley Byrne, application of, 17–18
DOGS,
  attacking livestock, strict liability
    for, 116–117
DUTY OF CARE. *See* CARE, DUTY OF

ECONOMIC LOSS,
  negligent acts,
    defective property, acquisition of,
      20–23
    generally, 19
    third party property, damage to,
      19–20
EMPLOYER'S LIABILITY,
  common law, at, 61–66
  delegation, 65–66
  master and servant. *See* MASTER AND
    SERVANT
  nature of duty,
    competent staff, 62–63
    generally, 62
    safe plant and equipment, 63–64

EMPLOYER'S LIABILITY—*cont.*
  safe premises, 65
  safe system of work, 64–65
  scope of duty, 65
ESCAPE,
  strict liability and, 106–107
EVIDENCE,
  negligence, of, 33–34
EX TURPI CAUSA,
  principle of, 51–52
EXAMINATION,
  intermediate, causation and, 59–60
EXAMINATIONS QUESTIONS AND ANSWER
    PLANS, 127–135
EXCLUSION NOTICE,
  occupier's liability and, 75
EXTRA-HAZARDOUS ACTIVITIES,
  vicarious liability for, 125

FAIR COMMENT,
  defamation, defence to action for,
    88–89
FALSE IMPRISONMENT,
  act of imprisonment, 4–6
  knowledge of plaintiff, 6
  meaning, 4
  means of escape, 6
FIRE,
  escape of, 111–112
FORSEEABILITY,
  duty of care, effect on, 11–12

GOODS,
  meaning, 53

Hedley Byrne,
  application of, 16–17
  care, duty of, 15–19
  contributory negligence, 17–18
  disclaimers, 17–18
  subsequent development, 15–16
  third party, reliance by, 18–19
HIGHWAY,
  nuisance on, 103–104
  operations on, vicarious liability for,
    124–125
  straying on, 118
HOSTILE,
  meaning, 1–2

IMPRISONMENT,
  act of, 4–6
  false. *See* FALSE IMPRISONMENT
  meaning, 4
INDEPENDENT CONTRACTORS,
  occupier's liability, 72–73
  vicarious liability,

INDEPENDENT CONTRACTORS—*cont.*
  casual negligence, 126
  collateral negligence, 126
  common law, 124–125
  generally, 124
  statutory duties, 125–126
INFIRM PERSON,
  contributory negligence, 46
INTENTIONAL PHYSICAL HARM,
  liability for, 7
INTERFERENCE. *See* NUISANCE
INTERMEDIATE EXAMINATION,
  causation and, 59–60
INTERVENING CAUSES,
  generally, 40–41
  natural force, 44
  plaintiff's intervention, 41–42
  third party, intervention by, 42–43

JUSTIFICATION,
  defamation, defence to action for, 87

KNOWLEDGE OF PLAINTIFF,
  false imprisonment, of, 6
  risk, of, 48

LAND,
  livestock straying on, 117–118
  neighbouring, withdrawal of support
    from, 124
  things brought on to, strict liability
    and, 106
LANDLORD,
  nuisance, liability for, 99–100
LEGAL IMMUNITIES,
  care, duty of, 27
LIABILITY,
  animals, for. *See* ANIMALS, LIABILITY
    FOR
  dangerous products, for. *See*
    DANGEROUS PRODUCTS
  employer, of. *See* EMPLOYER'S
    LIABILITY
  master and servant, joint liability of,
    123–124
  nuisance, for. *See* NUISANCE
  occupier, of. *See* OCCUPIER'S LIABILITY
  strict. *See* STRICT LIABILITY
  vicarious. *See* VICARIOUS LIABILITY
LIBEL,
  slander distinguished from, 82–83
LIVESTOCK,
  dogs attacking, 116–117
  straying,
    another's land, on, 117–118
    defences, 118
    detention of, 118

LIVESTOCK—*cont.*
  highway, on, 118
  sale of, 118
LOCALITY,
  unreasonable interference and
    nature of, 94–95

MANUFACTURER,
  dangerous products, liability for,
    58–59
  meaning, 59
MASTER AND SERVANT,
  course of employment, 121–123
  joint liability, 123–124
  lending servant, 120–121
  master's duty to servant, 125
  servant, meaning, 119–120
  vicarious liability, 119–124
MEANS OF ESCAPE,
  false imprisonment, effect on, 6
MISCHIEF,
  strict liability and, 106

NATURAL FORCE,
  intervening cause, as, 44
NECESSITY,
  trespass to person, defence to, 9
NEGLIGENCE,
  breach of duty,
    characteristics of defendant, 31–33
    evidence of negligence, 33–34
    reasonable man, 28–29
    risk, concept of, 29–31
  care, duty of,
    economic loss, 14–15
    establishing duty, 10–14
    generally, 10
    legal immunities, 27–28
    negligent acts, 19–23
    negligent mis–statement, 14–15
    nervous shock, 23–25
    omissions, 25–27
  casual, vicarious liability for,
    126
  causation,
    factual, 35–37
    generally, 35
  collateral, vicarious liability for, 126
  contributory. *See* CONTRIBUTORY
    NEGLIGENCE
  dangerous products, liability for,
    58–61
  evidence of, 33–34
  factual causation, 35–37
  intervening causes,
    generally, 40–41
    natural force, 44

NEGLIGENCE—*cont.*
  plaintiff's intervention, 41–42
  third party, intervention of, 42–43
  meaning, 10, 28
  proof of, 60–61
  remoteness of damage,
    competing tests, 37–38
    egg-shell skull rule, 39–40
    extent of damage, 39–40
    generally, 35
    manner of occurrence, 38
    type of damage, 38–39
NEGLIGENT ACT,
  economic loss caused by, 19–23
NERVOUS SHOCK,
  care, duty of, 23–25
  nature of, 23
NON-NATURAL USER,
  strict liability and, 107–108
NON-OCCUPIER,
  trespasser, liability to, 75–76
NUISANCE,
  coming to, 101
  defences,
    coming to nuisance, 101
    other defences, 101
    prescription, 100
    statutory authority, 100–101
  liability for,
    creator, 97
    landlord, 99–100
    occupier, 98–99
    standard of, 102–103
  nature of, 92
  private,
    damage, 97
    defences, 100–101
    generally, 92–93
    public nuisance distinguished
      from, 103
    remedies, 101–102
    standard of liability, 102–103
    unreasonable interference,
      93–97
    who can sue, 97
    who is liable, 97–100
  public,
    highway, on, 103–104
    nature of, 103
    private nuisance distinguished
      from, 103
  unreasonable interference,
    abnormal sensitivity, 95
    degree of interference, 94
    generally, 93–94
    intentional annoyance, 96–97
    locality, nature of, 94–95

NUISANCE—*cont.*
  social utility, 95
  state of affairs, 95–96

OCCUPIER'S LIABILITY,
  Act of 1957, 66–73
  Act of 1984, 73–76
  children, relating to, 71
  common duty of care,
    children, relating to, 71
    generally, 70
    independent contractors, relating
      to, 72–73
    special skills, relating to, 71–72
    warnings, 72
  damage, 73
  defences, 73
  exclusion notices, 75
  exclusion of duty, 69–70
  independent contractors, relating to,
    72–73
  nuisance, 98–99
  occupier, meaning, 66–67
  premises, 67
  scope of duty, 74–75
  special skills, 71–72
  trespasser, liability of non-occupier
    to, 75–76
  visitors, relating to, 67–69
  warnings, 72
OLD PERSON,
  contributory negligence, 46
OMISSIONS,
  care, duty of, 25–27
  exceptions to rule, 25–27

PARTIES,
  dangerous products, action relating
    to, 53–54
PASSENGERS. *See* CAR PASSENGERS
PERSON, TRESPASS TO. *See* TRESPASS TO
  PERSON
PERSONAL INJURY,
  strict liability and, 108
PHYSICAL FORCE,
  battery, application in case of, 1
PHYSICAL HARM,
  intentional, 7
PLAINTIFF,
  consent of, strict liability and, 110
  defamation of. *See* DEFAMATION
  default of, strict liability and, 110
  false imprisonment, knowledge of, 6
  intervention by, 41–42
  statutory duty owed to, 78
PLANT AND EQUIPMENT,
  safe, 63–64

PREMISES,
  occupier's liability, 67
  safe, 65
PRIVATE NUISANCE. *See* NUISANCE
PRIVILEGE,
  absolute, 89
  qualified, 90–91
PRODUCER,
  meaning, 53
PRODUCTS,
  dangerous. *See* DANGEROUS PRODUCTS
  meaning, 53–54
PROFESSIONAL,
  breach of duty of care, 32–33
PROOF,
  defamation, of,
    publication, 85–86
    reference to plaintiff, 85
    statement must be defamatory,
      83–85
  negligence, of, 60–61
  trespass to person, 1
PROPERTY,
  defective, acquisition of, 20–23
  third party, of, damage to, 19–20
PROXIMITY,
  duty of care, effect on, 11–12
PSYCHIATRIC DAMAGE. *See* NERVOUS
      SHOCK
PUBLIC NUISANCE. *See* NUISANCE
PUBLIC POLICY,
  ex turpi causa, 51–52
  just and reasonable requirements,
      12–13
PUBLICATION,
  defamation, proof of, 85–86

QUALIFIED PRIVILEGE,
  defamation, defence to action for,
      90–91

REASONABLE MAN,
  breach of duty, 28–29
REMEDIES,
  nuisance, action for, 101–102
REMOTENESS OF DAMAGE,
  competing tests, 37–38
  egg-shell skull rule, 39–40
  extent of damage, 39–40
  generally, 35
  manner of occurrence, 38
  type of damage, 38–39
RESCUERS,
  contributory negligence, 46
  volenti non fit injuria, 51
RISK,
  concept of, 29–31

RISK—*cont.*
  cost of precautions, 31
  magnitude of, 30
  plaintiff, knowledge of, 48
  social utility, 30–31

SAMPLE EXAMINATION QUESTIONS AND
      ANSWER PLANS, 127–135
SELF-DEFENCE,
  trespass to person, defence to, 9–10
SERVANT. *See* MASTER AND SERVANT
SLANDER,
  libel distinguished from, 82–83
SOCIAL UTILITY,
  risk, concept of, 30–31
  unreasonable interference and,
      95
SPECIAL SKILLS,
  occupier's liability, 71–72
SPORTING EVENTS,
  volenti non fit injuria, 49–50
STAFF,
  competent, 62–63
STATE OF AFFAIRS,
  unreasonable interference and,
      95–96
STATUTORY AUTHORITY,
  strict liability, defence to claim for,
      110
STATUTORY DUTY, BREACH OF,
  defences,
    contributory negligence, 81
    delegation, 81
    volenti non fit injuria, 81
  elements of tort,
    causation, 79–80
    damage of contemplated type,
      79
    defendant in breach of duty,
      78–79
    plaintiff, duty owed to, 78
  generally, 76
  right of action, whether intended,
      76–77
STRANGER, ACT OF,
  strict liability, defence to claim for,
      109–110
STRAYING LIVESTOCK. *See* LIVESTOCK
STRICT LIABILITY,
  dangerous animals, for,
    animals belonging to dangerous
      species, 113
    animals not belonging to
      dangerous species, 113–115
  defences to liability, 115–116
  generally, 112–113
  keeper, 115

STRICT LIABILITY—*cont.*
  defences,
    act of God, 109
    consent of plaintiff, 110
    dangerous animals, strict liability
      for, 115–116
    default of plaintiff, 110
    generally, 109
    statutory authority, 110
    stranger, act of, 109–110
  escape, 106–107
  fire, escape of,
    common law, 111
    statute, 111–112
  generally, 105
  land, things brought on to, 106
  likely to do mischief, 106
  non-natural user, 107–108
  personal injury, 108
  remoteness of damage, 108
  rule in *Rylands v. Fletcher*, 105–106

THIRD PARTY,
  intervention of, 42–43
  property, damage to, 19–20
  reliance by, 18–19
TRESPASS TO PERSON,
  assault,
    battery compared with, 3–4
    meaning, 3
  battery,
    examples, 2
    hostile, meaning, 1–2
    interference, nature of, 2–3
    meaning, 1
    physical force, application of, 1
  burden of proof, 1
  damages, 7
  defences,
    availability of, 8
    consent, 8–9
    contributory negligence, 9
    lawful arrest, 10
    necessity, 9
    self-defence, 9–10
  false imprisonment,
    act of imprisonment, 4–6
    knowledge of plaintiff, 6
    meaning, 4
    means of escape, 6
  intentional physical harm, 7
  nature of, 1

TRESPASSER,
  non-occupier, liability of, 75–76

ULTIMATE CONSUMER,
  meaning, 59
UNREASONABLE INTERFERENCE. *See*
  NUISANCE

VEHICLE OWNER,
  vicarious liability of, 126
VICARIOUS LIABILITY,
  common law,
    casual negligence, 126
    collateral negligence, 126
    extra-hazardous activities, 125
    highway, operations on, 124–125
    master's duty to servant, 125
    neighbouring land, withdrawal of
      support from, 124
    nuisance, 125
    other cases, 125
  generally, 119
  independent contractors,
    common law, 124–125
    generally, 124
  master and servant,
    course of employment, 121–123
    generally, 119
    joint liability, 123–124
    lending servant, 120–121
    servant, meaning, 119–120
  vehicle owners, 126
VISITORS,
  occupier's liability, 67–69
VOLENTI NON FIT INJURIA,
  agreement, 48–49
  car passengers, 50
  generally, 48
  knowledge of risk, 48
  particular cases, 49–51
  rescuers, 51
  sporting events, 49–50
  statutory duty, breach of, 81
  workmen, 50

WARNINGS,
  occupier's liability, 72
WORK,
  safe system of, 64–65
WORKMEN,
  contributory negligence, 46–47
  volenti non fit injuria, 50

Concept of Risk - Costs.

Have I exposed my Brother to
Unreasonable Harm

3 Factors examined.

a) Magnitude of Risk

B) Desirability of Conduct

C) Cost & Practeability of measures
to eliminate

(A)
Magnitude Risk

2 Factors law looks at.
Foreseeable. — Cricket Ball × Six 30 years
Degree of Harm: One eyed man.
                   Unscrewing Bolt
    Wm Case —   loses eye.
                 no goggles – But Risk great
B) Desirability of Activity
(C) Fire Engine lost case.